What People Are Saying about Threshold Bible Study

"The Threshold Bible Study connects the wisdom of God's word to our daily lives. This fine series will provide needed tools that can deepen your understanding of Scripture, but most importantly it can deepen your faith. In the classical tradition of lectio divina, this series also offers a very practical way to pray with Scripture, and I can think of nothing better for equipping people for the New Evangelization than a biblically soaked life of prayer."   Archbishop Charles J. Chaput, OFM Cap, Archbishop of Denver

"God's holy word addresses the deepest levels of our lives with the assurance of divine grace and wisdom for our individual and communal faith. I am grateful for this new series introducing our Catholic people to the riches of Sacred Scripture. May these guides to understanding the great truths of our Redemption bring us all closer to the Lord of our salvation."   Most Reverend Timothy M. Dolan, Archbishop of New York

"Threshold Bible Study successfully bridges the painful gap between solid biblical scholarship and the rich spiritual nourishment that we expect to find in the words of Scripture. In this way, indispensable biblical knowledge leads to that spiritual wisdom which enables us to live in accord with God's purposes. Stephen Binz is to be congratulated for responding to this urgent need in today's world."
Demetrius Dumm, OSB, professor of New Testament, Saint Vincent Seminary, Saint Vincent Archabbey, Latrobe, Pennsylvania

"Threshold Bible Study offers solid scholarship and spiritual depth. Drawing on the Church's living Tradition and the Jewish roots of the New Testament, Threshold Bible Study can be counted on for lively individual study and prayer, even while it offers spiritual riches to deepen communal conversation and reflection among the people of God."
Scott Hahn, Professor of biblical theology, Franciscan University of Steubenville

"Stephen Binz has an amazing gift for making the meaning of the biblical text come alive! With a strong background in Bible study, he knows how to provide the roadmap any group can use to explore Scripture. Using the method known as lectio divina, Threshold Bible Study provides two things: growth in understanding the sacred text, and at the same time, the opportunity for actual conversion as the text is broken open and shared. I'd like to put this into the hands of every adult Catholic in the church today."
Bill Huebsch, author and theologian, Director of PastoralPlanning.com

"Stephen Binz offers an invaluable guide that can make reading the Bible enjoyable (again) and truly nourishing. A real education on how to read the Bible, this series prepares people to discuss Scripture and to share it in community."

Jacques Nieuviarts, Professor of Scripture,
Institut Catholique de Toulouse, France

"The distance many feel between the word of God and their everyday lives can be overwhelming. It need not be so. Threshold Bible Study is a fine blend of the best of biblical scholarship and a realistic sensitivity to the spiritual journey of the believing Christian. I recommend it highly."

Francis J. Moloney, SDB,
Provincial Superior of the Salesians of Don Bosco in Australia,
Senior Fellow and professor of biblical studies at
Catholic Theological College, Melbourne College of Divinity

"Threshold Bible Study is appropriately named, for its commentary and study questions bring people to the threshold of the text and invite them in. The questions guide but do not dominate. They lead readers to ponder and wrestle with the biblical passages and take them across the threshold toward life with God. Stephen Binz's work stands in the tradition of the biblical renewal movement and brings it back to life. We need more of this in the Church."

Kathleen M. O'Connor, Professor of Old Testament,
Columbia Theological Seminary

"I most strongly recommend Stephen Binz's Threshold Bible Study for adult Bible classes, religious education, and personal spiritual enrichment. The series is exceptional for its scholarly solidity, pastoral practicality, and clarity of presentation. The church owes Binz a great debt of gratitude for his generous and competent labor in the service of the word of God."

Peter C. Phan, The Ignacio Ellacuria Professor of
Catholic Social Thought, Georgetown University

"Threshold Bible Study helpfully introduces the lay reader into the life-enhancing process of lectio divina or prayerful reading of scripture, individually or in a group. This series, prepared by a reputable biblical scholar and teacher, responds creatively to the exhortation of the Council to provide God's people abundant nourishment from the table of God's word. The process proposed leads the reader from Bible study to personal prayer, community involvement, and active Christian commitment in the world."

Sandra M. Schneiders, Professor of New Testament and Spirituality,
Jesuit School of Theology, Berkeley

"Threshold Bible Study unlocks the Scriptures and ushers the reader over the threshold into the world of God's living word. The world of the Bible comes alive with new meaning and understanding for our times. This series enables the reader to appreciate contemporary biblical scholarship and the meaning of God's word. This is the best material I have seen for serious Bible study."

Most Reverend Donald W. Trautman, Bishop of Erie

THRESHOLD
BIBLE STUDY

JESUS,
the WORD
MADE FLESH

PART ONE

John
[1–10]

STEPHEN J. BINZ

TWENTY
THIRD *23rd*
PUBLICATIONS

SECOND PRINTING 2016

TWENTY-THIRD PUBLICATIONS
A Division of Bayard
One Montauk Avenue, Suite 200
New London, CT 06320
(860) 437-3012 or (800) 321-0411
www.23rdpublications.com

ISBN 978-1-58595-828-3
Library of Congress Control Number: 2011923254
Printed in the U.S.A.

Contents

LESSONS 13–18

LESSONS 19–24

LESSONS 25–30

departments

Community Development Department

Aske operator when call

Records
Pub info

Smoke detector installation

City Counsel Chambers
Niles Fire Station
1345 E Main
City Administrator Ric Huff
Nicholas Shelton - 313 N. 2nd

1st Ward Gretchen Bertschy
Georgia Boggs
2nd Amanda Dunnem
Tim Rogers
3 William Weimer
Charlie McAfee
4 Michael Thompson
John DiCostanzo

Clerk Tina Bergman 333 N 2nd

2 + 4 Monday

Items are submitted by Mon noon
prior to a reg. Scheduled 2 or 4
6:00

Then set a date for public hearing
plan 2a 3 weeks 3 min

How to Use
Threshold Bible Study

Threshold Bible Study is a dynamic, informative, inspiring, and life-changing series that helps you learn about Scripture in a whole new way. Each book will help you explore new dimensions of faith and discover deeper insights for your life as a disciple of Jesus.

The threshold is a place of transition. The threshold of God's word invites you to enter that place where God's truth, goodness, and beauty can shine into your life and fill your mind and heart. Through the Holy Spirit, the threshold becomes holy ground, sacred space, and graced time. God can teach you best at the threshold, because God opens your life to his word and fills you with the Spirit of truth.

With Threshold Bible Study each topic or book of the Bible is approached in a thematic way. You will understand and reflect on the biblical texts through overarching themes derived from biblical theology. Through this method, the study of Scripture will impact your life in a unique way and transform you from within.

These books are designed for maximum flexibility. Each study is presented in a workbook format, with sections for reading, reflecting, writing, discussing, and praying. Each Threshold book contains thirty lessons, which you can use for your daily study over the course of a month or which can be divided into six lessons per week, providing a group study of six weekly sessions. These studies are ideal for Bible study groups, small Christian communities, adult faith formation, student groups, Sunday school, neighborhood groups, and family reading, as well as for individual learning.

The commentary that follows each biblical passage launches your reflection on that passage and helps you begin to see its significance within the context of your contemporary experience. The questions following the commentary challenge you to understand the passage more fully and apply it to your own life. Space for writing after each question is ideal for personal study and also allows group participants to prepare for the weekly discussion. The prayer helps conclude your study each day by integrating your learning into your relationship with God.

The method of Threshold Bible Study is rooted in the ancient tradition of *lectio divina*, whereby studying the Bible becomes a means of deeper intimacy with

God and a transformed life. Reading and interpreting the text (*lectio*) is followed by reflective meditation on its message (*meditatio*). This reading and reflecting flows into prayer from the heart (*oratio* and *contemplatio*). In this way, one listens to God through the Scripture and then responds to God in prayer.

This ancient method assures you that Bible study is a matter of both the mind and the heart. It is not just an intellectual exercise to learn more and be able to discuss the Bible with others. It is, more importantly, a transforming experience. Reflecting on God's word, guided by the Holy Spirit, illumines the mind with wisdom and stirs the heart with zeal.

Following the personal Bible study, Threshold Bible Study offers ways to extend personal *lectio divina* into a weekly conversation with others. This communal experience will allow participants to enhance their appreciation of the message and build up a spiritual community (*collatio*). The end result will be to increase not only individual faith but also faithful witness in the context of daily life (*operatio*).

When bringing Threshold Bible Study to a church community, try to make every effort to include as many people as possible. Many will want to study on their own; others will want to study with family, a group of friends, or a few work associates; some may want to commit themselves to share insights through a weekly conference call, daily text messaging, or an online social network; and others will want to gather weekly in established small groups.

By encouraging Threshold Bible Study and respecting the many ways people desire to make Bible study a regular part of their lives, you will widen the number of people in your church community who study the Bible regularly in whatever way they are able in their busy lives. Simply sign up people at the Sunday services and order bulk quantities for your church. Encourage people to follow the daily study as faithfully as they can through Sunday announcements, notices in parish publications, support on the church website, and other creative invitations and motivations.

Through the spiritual disciplines of Scripture reading, study, reflection, conversation, and prayer, Threshold Bible Study will help you experience God's grace more abundantly and root your life more deeply in Christ. The risen Jesus said: "Listen! I am standing at the door, knocking; if you hear my voice and open the door, I will come in to you and eat with you, and you with me" (Rev 3:20). Listen to the Word of God, open the door, and cross the threshold to an unimaginable dwelling with God!

SUGGESTIONS FOR INDIVIDUAL STUDY

• Make your Bible reading a time of prayer. Ask for God's guidance as you read the Scriptures.

• Try to study daily, or as often as possible according to the circumstances of your life.

• Read the Bible passage carefully, trying to understand both its meaning and its personal application as you read. Some persons find it helpful to read the passage aloud.

• Read the passage in another Bible translation. Each version adds to your understanding of the original text.

• Allow the commentary to help you comprehend and apply the scriptural text. The commentary is only a beginning, not the last word, on the meaning of the passage.

• After reflecting on each question, write out your responses. The very act of writing will help you clarify your thoughts, bring new insights, and amplify your understanding.

• As you reflect on your answers, think about how you can live God's word in the context of your daily life.

• Conclude each daily lesson by reading the prayer and continuing with your own prayer from the heart.

• Make sure your reflections and prayers are matters of both the mind and the heart. A true encounter with God's word is always a transforming experience.

• Choose a word or a phrase from the lesson to carry with you throughout the day as a reminder of your encounter with God's life-changing word.

• Share your learning experience with at least one other person whom you trust for additional insights and affirmation. The ideal way to share learning is in a small group that meets regularly.

SUGGESTIONS FOR GROUP STUDY

• Meet regularly; weekly is ideal. Try to be on time, and make attendance a high priority for the sake of the group. The average group meets for about an hour.

• Open each session with a prepared prayer, a song, or a reflection. Find some appropriate way to bring the group from the workaday world into a sacred time of graced sharing.

• If you have not been together before, name tags are very helpful as group members begin to become acquainted with one another.

• Spend the first session getting acquainted with one another, reading the Introduction aloud, and discussing the questions that follow.

• Appoint a group facilitator to provide guidance to the discussion. The role of facilitator may rotate among members each week. The facilitator simply keeps the discussion on track; each person shares responsibility for the group. There is no need for the facilitator to be a trained teacher.

• Try to study the six lessons on your own during the week. When you have done your own reflection and written your own answers, you will be better prepared to discuss the six scriptural lessons with the group. If you have not had an opportunity to study the passages during the week, meet with the group anyway to share support and insights.

• Participate in the discussion as much as you are able, offering your thoughts, insights, feelings, and decisions. You learn by sharing with others the fruits of your study.

• Be careful not to dominate the discussion. It is important that everyone in the group be offered an equal opportunity to share the results of their work. Try to link what you say to the comments of others so that the group remains on the topic.

• When discussing your own personal thoughts or feelings, use "I" language. Be as personal and honest as appropriate, and be very cautious about giving advice to others.

• Listen attentively to the other members of the group so as to learn from their insights. The words of the Bible affect each person in a different way, so a group provides a wealth of understanding for each member.

• Don't fear silence. Silence in a group is as important as silence in personal study. It allows individuals time to listen to the voice of God's Spirit and the opportunity to form their thoughts before they speak.

• Solicit several responses for each question. The thoughts of different people will build on the answers of others and will lead to deeper insights for all.

• Don't fear controversy. Differences of opinions are a sign of a healthy and honest group. If you cannot resolve an issue, continue on, agreeing to disagree. There is probably some truth in each viewpoint.

• Discuss the questions that seem most important for the group. There is no need to cover all the questions in the group session.

• Realize that some questions about the Bible cannot be resolved, even by experts. Don't get stuck on some issue for which there are no clear answers.

• Whatever is said in the group is said in confidence and should be regarded as such.

• Pray as a group in whatever way feels comfortable. Pray for the members of your group throughout the week.

Schedule for Group Study

Session 1: Introduction   Date: _____

Session 2: Lessons 1–6   Date: _____

Session 3: Lessons 7–12   Date: _____

Session 4: Lessons 13–18   Date: _____

Session 5: Lessons 19–24   Date: _____

Session 6: Lessons 25–30   Date: _____

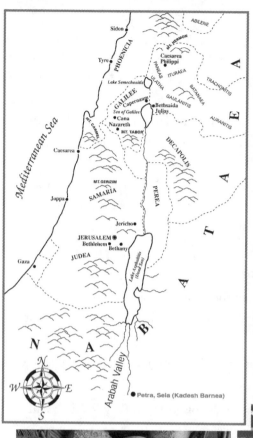

**And the Word became flesh and lived among us,
and we have seen his glory, the glory as of a father's only son,
full of grace and truth.** John 1:14

Jesus, the Word Made Flesh (Part 1)

Throughout the ages, through endless varieties of religions and systems of belief, human beings have sought to encounter God. The evidence of religious expressions—temples, rituals, and sacred writings in every corner of the world in every age of history—convince us that this search to experience God is the deepest longing of the human condition. Yet the many attempts by all religions to meet God have only resulted in brief glimpses and fleeting insights into God's full reality. Ultimately, God is absolutely transcendent, so different from us and so far beyond us that human words and the human senses are incapable of grasping God's essence. The tradition of the Hebrew Scriptures expresses this transcendence of God by stating in various ways that God cannot be seen by human beings. God says in Exodus, "No one shall see me and live" (Exod 33:20).

Yet the gospel according to John demonstrates that humanity has reached a new experience in its attempt to encounter God. It announces that Jesus himself is the revelation of God, that if we want to know the unseen God, we must look intently at Jesus. "No one has ever seen God," the last line of the Gospel prologue confirms. But the way to meet God is through the life of

1

God's Son: "It is God the only Son, who is close to the Father's heart, who has made him known" (John 1:18).

This is the key to the fourth gospel. John announces that the revelation brought by Jesus, the Son of God made flesh, makes possible a genuine and definitive knowledge of God. The Son is able to reveal God to us because he has lived with the Father throughout eternity. The Son has forever been "close to the Father's heart." The expression "close to the Father's heart" suggests an intimate relationship that unites Jesus inseparably to the Father in a bond of tender love.

This eternal bond of the Son with the Father enables Jesus to reveal God to us. And because the bond of the Father and the Son is one of intimate love, the revelation that Jesus offers us is not just one of doctrines about God but rather of letting the Father shine through his earthly life. As Jesus reveals himself, through the actions and teachings of his life among us, he shows us the Father. As Jesus proclaimed at the end of his public life: "Whoever sees me sees him who sent me" (12:45).

Reflection and Discussion

• In what ways have I sought to encounter God? Why do these give me only partial glimpses and insights into God's full reality?

• What does John's gospel tell us is unique about the revelation of God in Jesus? In what ways does this alter my attempts to encounter God?

Revelation through Signs and Divine Titles

One of the ways that Jesus reveals God to us is through the "signs" of John's gospel. The narrative contains a series of "signs," the word John uses to designate the wondrous deeds of Jesus. The author chose those miracles of Jesus that were most used in the preaching of the church. And rather than simply recounting these miracles and letting them speak for themselves, John developed them into great dramas, and they became powerful stories to teach about who Jesus is.

The first eleven chapters of the gospel recount seven signs: first, changing water into wine at Cana (2:1–11); second, healing the royal official's son (4:46–54); third, healing the paralyzed man at the pool (5:1–15); fourth, feeding the five thousand with the loaves and fish (6:1–15); fifth, walking on the water (6:16–21); sixth, healing the blind man (9:1–41); and seventh, raising Lazarus from the dead (11:1–44). These deeds of healing and power are not so much significant in and of themselves as in their ability to point beyond themselves. Each of these seven signs points to the truth about who Jesus is. They are important because they reveal the Father at work in Jesus. They manifest the power and the love of God as Jesus draws people into the Father's heart.

In each of these signs, the emphasis is placed on the meaning of the event and the spiritual reality of the miracle. When Jesus cures a sick person, the gospel makes it clear that this is a complete healing, a healing of the body and the spirit. When Jesus restores the sight of the blind man, the dialogue that follows makes it clear that Jesus has also given him spiritual sight (in contrast to the blindness of the Pharisees). When Jesus gives physical life to Lazarus, it is an outward manifestation of the eternal life Jesus gives to all. Physical health, sight, and life are gifts that anticipate God's total healing, true vision, and eternal life. These gifts that Jesus offers are manifestations of the life that God wants to give to all people as they encounter him through the life of his Son.

Our transcendent, unseen God has always manifested himself through "signs" to his people, beginning in the foundational event of salvation history, the exodus. These Old Testament stories form the background for much of the Gospel of John. The Passover lamb, bronze serpent, manna, water from the rock, crossing the sea, the authority of Moses—all of these are ancient exodus motifs that form the context for the revelation of Jesus. In Exodus we are told that God multiplied "signs" through Moses, but the people refused to believe. In the book of Numbers God asked: "How long will they refuse to believe in me, in spite of all the signs I have done among them?" (Num 14:11). Like the signs God worked through Moses, the signs in John's gospel are works of revelation. They are actions of God that liberate people and lead them to salvation. Yet, as in the case of Moses, the gospel notes, "Although he had performed so many signs in their presence, they did not believe in him" (12:37).

A sign is an encounter with God and is intended to lead people to faith. John wrote his gospel to help us come to faith in Jesus Christ, because faith leads to life. He states his purpose very clearly toward the end of the gospel: "Now Jesus did many other signs in the presence of his disciples that are not written in this book. But these are written so that you may come to believe that Jesus is the Messiah, the Son of God, and that through believing you may have life in his name" (20:30–31). Thus, the most important reaction we should have when reading the gospel is a response of faith. We read not just for information or doctrinal knowledge, but to encounter the living Christ so that he may reveal to us the life of the Father and draw us near to his heart.

Another way that the Gospel of John reveals God to us through Jesus is through the "I am" sayings. On several occasions throughout the gospel, Jesus identifies himself with the words "I am." For anyone familiar with the Old Testament, the words "I am" immediately call to mind God's encounter with Moses at the burning bush. For example, Jesus solemnly declared: "Very truly, I tell you, before Abraham was, I am" (8:58). By claiming this divine title for Jesus, the gospel writer expresses the oneness of Jesus with the Father, so much so that those who encounter Jesus also experience the unseen God.

There are also seven instances in the gospel in which Jesus speaks of himself with the phrase "I am..." followed by a variety of different predicates: "I am the bread of life" (6:35); "I am the light of the world" (8:12); "I am the gate for the sheep" (10:7); "I am the good shepherd" (10:11); "I am the resurrection and the life" (11:25); "I am the way, and the truth, and the life" (14:6); and "I am the true vine" (15:1). The predicate is a description of who Jesus is in relationship to us. The seven images, like the seven "signs," are keys to understanding the nature of Jesus and his work in the world. They proclaim that Jesus himself, present in flesh in our concrete world, is truly the definitive revelation of the Father.

Reflection and Discussion

• What is the difference between a "sign" in John's gospel and a miracle in the other gospels?

• Why is a familiarity with the Old Testament so helpful in understanding John's gospel?

The Physical, Earthly Revelation of God

Sometimes the Gospel of John is described as a "spiritual" gospel. While it is true that this gospel emphasizes the divine and other-worldly nature of Christ, it also makes it very clear that Jesus was a physical being who manifested the presence of God in very concrete, earthly ways. Throughout the gospel his humanity is unmistakable. Jesus knows the weariness of a tired body and the powerful emotions of the human heart. He was angry in the temple courts; he was tired as he sat down at the well in Samaria; he visibly wept at the death of his friend; he cried out on the cross with parched lips, "I am thirsty."

The gospel also sets this human Jesus in a very real, physical world. The gospel indicates a detailed knowledge of the geography of Palestine, its regions and peoples. The author writes in amazingly accurate detail about the city of Jerusalem: for example, the sheep gate and the pool of Bethesda, the pool of Siloam, Solomon's portico, the stone pavement of Pilate's praetorium, and Golgotha, which he says looks like a skull. Much of the gospel reads like that of an eyewitness, giving us many details that enhance our experience of Jesus living within the historical reality of his times.

The Gospel of John, even more than the other gospels, is filled with vivid, dramatic scenes in which Jesus personally encounters a host of other human beings. He encounters John the Baptist and his first disciples (chapter 1), his mother at Cana (chapter 2), Nicodemus (chapter 3), the Samaritan woman (chapter 4), the royal official (chapter 4), the paralyzed man at the pool (chapter 5), and many others. Through these human experiences, Jesus enables people to "see" the Father. In response to Philip's request that Jesus "show" him the Father, Jesus said, "Have I been with you all this time, Philip, and you still do not know me? Whoever has seen me has seen the Father" (14:9). Jesus reveals God through human encounters, not so much through communicating beliefs but through experiences of the senses—as John said in the opening words of his first letter: "what we have heard, what we have seen with our eyes, what we have looked at and touched with our hands" (1 John 1:1). By revealing himself in earthly life, Jesus makes the Father known.

More than any other gospel, this proclamation of the good news summarizes the reason why the Christian religion is incarnational. All the good news of Christianity springs forth from the climactic verse of John's prologue: "The Word became flesh and lived among us, and we have seen his glory, the glory as of a father's only son, full of grace and truth" (1:14). The eternal Word of God became human; he literally pitched his tent in our world. This image of the tent is a metaphor from the exodus for God's dwelling among his people in the wilderness. God's "glory" is the visible manifestation of his majesty, seen in the desert and Jerusalem's temple, and now in the very person of Jesus Christ. It is this wondrous reality of God incarnate among us that radiates throughout the whole gospel, filling it with light and wonder.

Reflection and Discussion

• In what ways does John's gospel emphasize both the divine and human natures of Jesus?

• How does the Incarnation make the Christian religion unique among all other systems of belief? How does John's gospel make this dogma personal and real?

The One-of-a-Kind Gospel

The four gospels share many common elements. They tell of Jesus' inspiring words and powerful deeds as he traveled from Galilee to Jerusalem. They recount many similar stories, like the feeding of the crowds, the healing of blindness, and the events surrounding the crucifixion of Jesus. By recalling his words and deeds, the power of his presence, and the impact of this experience on their lives, the early disciples began to form the memories and expressions of faith from which the gospels were eventually written. The very end of the fourth gospel reminds us that the account is only a limited view of Jesus, only a fraction of all that could be said about him, only a segment of all his many words and deeds. John concludes: "There are also many other things that Jesus did; if every one of them were written down, I suppose that the world itself could not contain the books that would be written" (21:25).

Though each of the four gospels creates a unique expression of who Jesus is, the Gospel of John stands out as significantly different from the rest. With its rich symbolism, its unique vocabulary, its developed theology, and its spiritual insight, this fourth gospel bears only superficial resemblance to the gospels of Matthew, Mark, and Luke. In fact, ninety percent of the material of the other gospels is simply not found in John. His gospel does not contain parables, nor do we see Jesus performing exorcisms. Unlike the other gospels, we do not find in John any rapid accounts of miracles; rather we have seven carefully chosen miracles which become teaching moments. Whereas in Matthew, Mark, and Luke, the central message of Jesus was the kingdom of God, in the Gospel of John, Jesus proclaims himself. In the series of "I am" statements, Jesus reveals who he is in a style that reflects God's self-revelation in the Old Testament. At the Last Supper John does not give an account of the institution of Eucharist, rather he narrates Jesus washing his disciples' feet. And the passion and death of Jesus, which is presented in the other gospels as Jesus' self-humiliation, is presented in John's gospel as a process of glorification. And, perhaps most dramatically, the gospel does not begin with Jesus' baptism or with infancy accounts. Rather, the beginning of this gospel takes us back before the world was created, to the Son's existence with God from all eternity.

Though the authorship and origin of the fourth gospel are frequently disputed and discussed, there is no significant reason to doubt the opinion of second-century theologians and historians that John the Apostle was its source. According to these writers, John lived to a ripe old age and was the last of the evangelists to write his gospel. Because he lived in Ephesus, the churches of Asia Minor were probably the first to hear this gospel proclaimed, though John no doubt envisioned an eventual audience that was more universal. Though some question the ability of a Galilean fisherman to create the literary artistry of this gospel, he was most likely assisted by more educated scribes, and his gospel could have been edited from more primitive forms during the final decades of the first century. Whatever the details of its origin, God's Spirit has produced a magnificent testimony of apostolic witness and ecclesial faith.

Reflection and Discussion

• What might be some reasons why John's gospel is so significantly different from the others?

• What are some of the unique ways the Gospel of John might lead me to appreciate the person of Jesus?

Prayer

Creator God, you are the loving source of all that exists and you have renewed the world through the coming of the Word Made Flesh. Through the words of this holy gospel, deepen my belief that Jesus is the Messiah and Son of God so that through believing I may have life in his name. Shine your light into my mind and heart, and give me a desire to know Jesus Christ more fully and to love others as he loves. Help me to respond to his invitation to "come and see," and encourage me to remain faithful to the challenges of study and prayer which your word offers me.

SUGGESTIONS FOR FACILITATORS, GROUP SESSION 1

1. If the group is meeting for the first time, or if there are newcomers joining the group, it is helpful to provide nametags.

2. Distribute the books to the members of the group.

3. You may want to ask the participants to introduce themselves and tell the group a bit about themselves.

4. Ask one or more of these introductory questions:
   - What drew you to join this group?
   - What is your biggest fear in beginning this Bible study?
   - How is beginning this study like a "threshold" for you?

5. You may want to pray this prayer as a group:

Come upon us, Holy Spirit, to enlighten and guide us as we begin this study of John's gospel. You inspired the writers of the Scriptures to reveal your presence throughout the history of salvation. This inspired word has the power to convert our hearts and change our lives. Fill our hearts with desire, trust, and confidence as you shine the light of your truth within us. Motivate us to read the Scriptures, and give us a deeper love for God's word each day. Bless us during this session and throughout the coming week with the fire of your love.

6. Read the Introduction aloud, pausing at each question for discussion. Group members may wish to write the insights of the group as each question is discussed. Encourage several members of the group to respond to each question.

7. Don't feel compelled to finish the complete Introduction during the session. It is better to allow sufficient time to talk about the questions raised than to rush to the end. Group members may read any remaining sections on their own after the group meeting.

8. Instruct group members to read the first six lessons on their own during the six days before the next group meeting. They should write out their own answers to the questions as preparation for next week's group discussion.

9. Fill in the date for each group meeting under "Schedule for Group Study."

10. Conclude by praying aloud together the prayer at the end of the Introduction.

The true light, which enlightens everyone, was coming into the world.
John 1:9

The Incarnation
of the Divine Word

JOHN 1:1–18 ¹*In the beginning was the Word, and the Word was with God, and the Word was God.* ²*He was in the beginning with God.* ³*All things came into being through him, and without him not one thing came into being. What has come into being* ⁴*in him was life, and the life was the light of all people.* ⁵*The light shines in the darkness, and the darkness did not overcome it.*
⁶*There was a man sent from God, whose name was John.* ⁷*He came as a witness to testify to the light, so that all might believe through him.* ⁸*He himself was not the light, but he came to testify to the light.* ⁹*The true light, which enlightens everyone, was coming into the world.*

¹⁰*He was in the world, and the world came into being through him; yet the world did not know him.* ¹¹*He came to what was his own, and his own people did not accept him.* ¹²*But to all who received him, who believed in his name, he gave power to become children of God,* ¹³*who were born, not of blood or of the will of the flesh or of the will of man, but of God.*

¹⁴*And the Word became flesh and lived among us, and we have seen his glory, the glory as of a father's only son, full of grace and truth.*

¹⁵*(John testified to him and cried out, "This was he of whom I said, 'He who comes after me ranks ahead of me because he was before me.'")* ¹⁶*From his full-*

ness we have all received, grace upon grace. [17] *The law indeed was given through Moses; grace and truth came through Jesus Christ.* [18] *No one has ever seen God. It is God the only Son, who is close to the Father's heart, who has made him known.*

This gospel begins by taking us back long before Bethlehem, even before creation, to the realm of timeless eternity. The phrase "in the beginning" echoes the opening of the Bible's first book (Gen 1:1). "The Word" conveys the idea of divine self-expression. A human word is, in a sense, the extension of a person into his environment; the divine Word is God's reaching out, seeking to share his divine being, sharing eternal love with creation. A human word reveals hidden thoughts; the divine Word reveals the hidden nature of God, demonstrating that God is loving, caring, and forgiving.

Since the Word existed in the beginning, one might think that either "the Word was God" or "the Word was with God." John affirms both (verses 1–2). The text suggests a distinction between the Word and God, but not a separation. Everything came into being through the Word. God's Word began to be known first through creation, then through the Torah and prophets of Israel, and finally through Jesus Christ. As God's self-expression, "the Word" encompasses Jesus' entire ministry, showing that all his words and works flow from his eternal existence and God's self-manifestation in salvation history.

In Jesus Christ, "the Word became flesh" (verse 14). The eternal Word has been born into frail humanity. In the Word Made Flesh, God has chosen to be with his people in a more personal way than ever before. John shows that the incarnation is on a scale with the creation of the world. In this new creation, the incarnate Word gives to humanity the power to become children of God, to be reborn, not of natural descent or human initiative, but of God (verse 13). This is the ultimate reason why the Word became flesh: so that we might be raised up to share intimately in God's life. John's gospel is an invitation to share in that new life. The tragedy of the gospel is that many fail to recognize and receive the Word, the source of life and light.

This prologue to John's gospel introduces a number of themes that originate in the Old Testament and will be further developed through the gospel. Though "no one has ever seen God" (verse 18), not even Moses, we have seen the "glory" of God's Word—a manifestation of God's presence in a way that we can understand (verse 14). He is the "true light" (verse 9) that shines in the darkness of sin and ignorance, and this shining glory enables us to see God reflected in Jesus and to share in his life. In the incarnate Word, God "lived among us." Literally, he pitched his tent, taking up residence among his people in a way far more intimate than when God dwelt in the tabernacle of the wilderness or in the temple of Jerusalem. He is the fullness of all the "grace and truth" God gave to Israel in the past, and "from his fullness we have all received, grace upon grace" (verse 16). Through grace was indeed given through Moses and the law, "grace upon grace"—the final grace, an everlasting and rapid succession of blessings, the ultimate grace—is given through Jesus Christ.

Reflection and Discussion

• How are my words the extension of myself to others? Am I a person of my word? Do I honor the power of my words for the sake of others?

• In what ways does John's prologue recall the creation account at the beginning of the Bible? How does the prologue introduce Jesus as a new creation?

• In what sense can we say that "grace and truth came through Jesus Christ"?

• John makes it clear that the Word did not become manifest merely as an apparition, but truly "became flesh and lived among us." What difference does this divine "enfleshment" mean for my life?

• Read the prologue again aloud, noticing the phrases that form the gospel's themes. In what way does the last verse launch you into the remainder of the gospel?

Prayer

Word of God, you shine in the world and enlighten my life. Cast out the darkness of falsehood and ignorance; show me the truth, love, and goodness of God. Open my heart to the grace upon grace that I will experience through this gospel.

**"I am the voice of one crying out in the wilderness,
'Make straight the way of the Lord.'"** John 1:23

The Mission of John the Baptist

JOHN 1:19–28 ¹⁹*This is the testimony given by John when the Jews sent priests and Levites from Jerusalem to ask him, "Who are you?"* ²⁰*He confessed and did not deny it, but confessed, "I am not the Messiah."* ²¹*And they asked him, "What then? Are you Elijah?" He said, "I am not." "Are you the prophet?" He answered, "No."* ²²*Then they said to him, "Who are you? Let us have an answer for those who sent us. What do you say about yourself?"* ²³*He said,*

"I am the voice of one crying out in the wilderness,
'Make straight the way of the Lord,'" as the prophet Isaiah said.

²⁴*Now they had been sent from the Pharisees.* ²⁵*They asked him, "Why then are you baptizing if you are neither the Messiah, nor Elijah, nor the prophet?"* ²⁶*John answered them, "I baptize with water. Among you stands one whom you do not know,* ²⁷*the one who is coming after me; I am not worthy to untie the thong of his sandal."* ²⁸*This took place in Bethany across the Jordan where John was baptizing.*

As in the other gospels, John's gospel links the beginnings of Jesus' ministry with the work of John the Baptist. Mention has already been made of him in the prologue: "There was a man sent from God whose name was John" (verse 6). He was sent "as a witness to testify to the light" (verse 7), though "he himself was not the light" (verse 8). The gospel presents the "witness" and "testimony" of John the Baptist as if readers were witnessing a trial scene, with evidence being presented to be evaluated by the court.

The authorities in Jerusalem send emissaries to interrogate John, asking him, "Who are you?" (verse 19). John's reply emphatically states who he is not: "I am not the Messiah" (verse 20). The envoys then suggest that if he is not the Messiah he might be one of the expected precursor figures. Elijah, who had never died but was taken up in a chariot of fire and a whirlwind into heaven (2 Kings 2:11), was expected to return before the day of the Lord (Mal 4:5). The prophet was a figure predicted by Moses who was expected to usher in the messianic era (Deut 18:15). John seemed to have the demeanor of a prophet, and his rugged lifestyle and powerful message made the questions of the emissaries seem appropriate. Yet, John denies being any of these messianic or end-time figures.

Frustrated by John's denials, the delegation from Jerusalem demands a positive identification: "What do you say about yourself?" (verse 22). John describes himself as "a voice" directing people to Jesus, the Word. Applying the words of Isaiah to himself, John identifies himself as "the voice crying out in the wilderness" (see Isa 40:3). He presents himself as the herald of a new exodus, announcing that God is about to redeem his people from bondage, as in the days of Moses. Like the prophets of old, John's ministry was preparatory for the imminent work of God. "Make straight the way of the Lord" evokes an image of preparing a roadway by clearing away the obstacles. In its original context, the passage was a call to prepare the way for God's people to leave the captivity of their exile in Babylon and return to Jerusalem. John the Baptist recognized it as a call to prepare the people of Israel for the redeeming work of the Messiah.

The delegation then demands to know, "Why then are you baptizing?" (verse 25), assuming that one offering baptism and repentance as the way to escape final judgment must be a messianic figure. John defers his answer and shifts the focus to the one who is not yet known to his questioners, "the one who is coming after me" (verse 27). The way is set for the Coming One, the one whose sandal thong a figure as great as John the Baptist was not worthy to untie. The important question of the gospel is not who John is, but who Jesus is.

Reflection and Discussion

• How does John the Baptist see his own role in relationship to that of Jesus?

• John the Baptist understands his role as clearing away the obstacles that prevent people from coming to Jesus. What obstacles get in the way today?

• If officials from Jerusalem were sent to me and asked, "Who are you?" how would I respond? In what sense is my response like or unlike that of John?

Prayer

Lord Jesus, you are the Coming One for whom the ministry of John the Baptist prepared. As I prepare my heart for you, help me to clear away the obstacles and make straight the way of your coming.

"He on whom you see the Spirit descend and remain is the one who baptizes with the Holy Spirit." John 1:33

The Lamb of God Who Takes Away the Sin of the World

JOHN 1:29–34 *²⁹The next day he saw Jesus coming toward him and declared, "Here is the Lamb of God who takes away the sin of the world! ³⁰This is he of whom I said, 'After me comes a man who ranks ahead of me because he was before me.' ³¹I myself did not know him; but I came baptizing with water for this reason, that he might be revealed to Israel." ³²And John testified, "I saw the Spirit descending from heaven like a dove, and it remained on him. ³³I myself did not know him, but the one who sent me to baptize with water said to me, 'He on whom you see the Spirit descend and remain is the one who baptizes with the Holy Spirit.' ³⁴And I myself have seen and have testified that this is the Son of God."*

John the Baptist continues his role as a witness testifying to the light (verse 8). On the day before, John had testified about himself in relationship to Jesus. In this scene, John provides direct testimony about Jesus as he sees him coming toward him. John confesses Jesus to be both the Lamb of God (verse 29) and the Son of God (verse 34). He answers the question that he had deferred the day before, "Why are you baptizing?" His baptizing is for the sake of Jesus, "that he might be revealed to Israel" (verse 31).

John first identifies Jesus as "the Lamb of God who takes away the sin of the world." He is not just any lamb; he is "the" Lamb, the Lamb par excellence. And he is God's Lamb, the Lamb whom God has provided for sacrifice to take away the world's sin. The origin of the title reaches back to Abraham who, when his son Isaac was carrying the wood for his own sacrifice on his back, assured him, "God himself will provide the lamb" (Gen 22:8). John was also thinking about the Suffering Servant from the prophecies of Isaiah. God's Servant would bear the iniquities of others and offer himself "like a lamb that is led to the slaughter" (Isa 53:7).

The title "Lamb of God" anticipates the passion narrative in which Jesus will be described as the fulfillment of the Passover lamb, which God commanded Israel to sacrifice as a memorial of their liberation from bondage (Exod 12). The Lamb whom God provides will atone for sins through his sacrificial death, liberating his people from the bondage of sin. Moreover, the Lamb of God will take upon himself not only the sin of Israel, but of the entire world. The work of this Lamb is many-sided. He is not simply a victim, but the Savior of the world. He is the one through whom God will forgive the sin of all humanity and reconcile the world to himself.

John testifies that he did not know Jesus when he began baptizing with water. Then God revealed Jesus to him: "He on whom you see the Spirit descend and remain is the one who baptizes with the Holy Spirit" (verse 33). The gospel does not narrate Jesus' baptism by John, as do the other gospels; and it is at this event in those gospels that the Spirit descended upon Jesus. Here the gospel notes that the Spirit descended on Jesus not only temporary—as the Spirit had come upon certain individuals in the Old Testament to empower them for a particular task—but that the Spirit remained on Jesus, marking his whole ministry with divine anointing as Israel's Messiah. Unlike John the Baptist, Jesus will baptize with the Holy Spirit. He will not only be the bearer of the Spirit but also the dispenser of the Spirit, effecting the reality for which John's water baptism only prepared the way.

The revelation to which John testifies shows the divine relationship between the Father, Son, and Holy Spirit. The Father has sent his Son as the Word Made Flesh and sent the Holy Spirit to dwell in him. As the Son of God, Jesus will bestow the Spirit on all people in the last days, as the Father has promised, through the prophets. The title Son of God evokes the intimate relationship between Jesus and his heavenly Father, the depth of which will be continually explored throughout the gospel.

Reflection and Discussion

• Why is the title "Lamb of God" such an ideal image for describing the redemptive work of Jesus?

• The gospel has already bestowed upon Jesus a number of titles: the Word, the Light, the Messiah, the Lamb of God, the Son of God. Why is Jesus given such a variety of names or titles? Which one of these most attracts me for further exploration?

• How am I called to be a witness to Jesus Christ? What is the content of my testimony? What does John the Baptist teach me about effective witnessing?

Prayer

Lamb of God, you have taken away my sin and that of the whole world. Give me the desire to know you more completely. Send your Spirit upon me so that I may be an effective witness to you in word and in deed.

"We have found him about whom Moses in the law and also the prophets wrote, Jesus son of Joseph from Nazareth." John 1:45

Jesus Calls His First Disciples

JOHN 1:35–51 [35]*The next day John again was standing with two of his disciples,* [36]*and as he watched Jesus walk by, he exclaimed, "Look, here is the Lamb of God!"* [37]*The two disciples heard him say this, and they followed Jesus.* [38]*When Jesus turned and saw them following, he said to them, "What are you looking for?" They said to him, "Rabbi" (which translated means Teacher), "where are you staying?"* [39]*He said to them, "Come and see." They came and saw where he was staying, and they remained with him that day. It was about four o'clock in the afternoon.* [40]*One of the two who heard John speak and followed him was Andrew, Simon Peter's brother.* [41]*He first found his brother Simon and said to him, "We have found the Messiah" (which is translated Anointed).* [42]*He brought Simon to Jesus, who looked at him and said, "You are Simon son of John. You are to be called Cephas" (which is translated Peter).*

[43]*The next day Jesus decided to go to Galilee. He found Philip and said to him, "Follow me."* [44]*Now Philip was from Bethsaida, the city of Andrew and Peter.* [45]*Philip found Nathanael and said to him, "We have found him about whom Moses in the law and also the prophets wrote, Jesus son of Joseph from Nazareth."* [46]*Nathanael said to him, "Can anything good come out of Nazareth?" Philip said to him, "Come and see."* [47]*When Jesus saw Nathanael coming toward him, he*

said of him, "Here is truly an Israelite in whom there is no deceit!" ⁴⁸Nathanael asked him, "Where did you get to know me?" Jesus answered, "I saw you under the fig tree before Philip called you." ⁴⁹Nathanael replied, "Rabbi, you are the Son of God! You are the King of Israel!" ⁵⁰Jesus answered, "Do you believe because I told you that I saw you under the fig tree? You will see greater things than these." ⁵¹And he said to him, "Very truly, I tell you, you will see heaven opened and the angels of God ascending and descending upon the Son of Man."

Narrated in a series of consecutive days, the gospel demonstrates that John the Baptist came as a witness to testify to the light. On the first day, John presents himself in contrast to the light (verses 19–28). On the second day, he bears witness to the light (verses 29–34). On the third day, he brings others to the light by pointing his disciples to Jesus (verses 35–42). On the fourth day, Jesus has stepped out of the shadow of John the Baptist, and the light begins to shine in the world (verses 43–51).

John again announces that Jesus is the Lamb of God. But this time he confesses this truth to two of his own disciples (verses 35–36). This marks the end of John's role in salvation history, and these two disciples begin to follow Jesus. In this gospel, disciples of Jesus usually either come to him on their own, or they are brought to Jesus through the efforts of another. In the case of these first two disciples, we see that John the Baptist is not only a crucial witness to Jesus but also the source from which Jesus drew his first followers.

The invitation to discipleship, like nearly every incident in John's gospel, contains multiple levels of meaning. The apparently casual question asked by Jesus of those following him, "What are you looking for?" (verse 38), is also probing and challenging. Jesus is really asking them if they know what they are searching for, if they know the meaning and purpose of their lives. We must realize that Jesus is also asking us the same question, as we seek to enter a deeper relationship with Jesus through this gospel.

Likewise, the question of the disciples, "Where are you staying?" (verse 38), and the response of Jesus, "Come and see" (verse 39), are an inquiry about the residence of this new teacher and an invitation to his home. But at the more profound level, the disciples are asking Jesus about his true home, where his heart is rooted, and Jesus invites them to come and experience his life, to abide with him and learn from him so that they can discover the truth about

God's love. The same invitation is ours, as we respond to the invitation to follow Jesus and experience his life.

The first precondition of discipleship is a profound yearning for deeper life. Jesus sees in these disciples not only who they are now, but the persons they will become. Jesus looks at Simon and sees that he will become Cephas, the Rock (verse 42). He looks at Nathaniel and sees "an Israelite in whom there is no deceit" (verse 48). Andrew, Simon Peter, Philip, and Nathaniel are all invited to "come and see." They come to know that Jesus too is more than he appears. On the surface Jesus is the "son of Joseph from Nazareth" (verse 45), but he is also the Lamb of God (verse 36), the Messiah (verse 41), the one about whom Moses and the prophets wrote (verse 45), the Son of God and King of Israel (verse 49).

Jesus promises these early disciples that they have far more to experience and comprehend: "Very truly, I tell you, you will see heaven opened and the angels of God ascending and descending upon the Son of Man" (verse 51). Jesus alludes to Jacob's dream of the ladder reaching to heaven, with the angels ascending and descending upon it (Gen 28:12), assuring Jacob of God's fidelity. Jesus is telling his disciples that he himself is the place where God is revealed, where heaven and earth are joined, where God and humankind meet. Jesus is the culmination of divine revelation: He provides a fullness of God's self-disclosure about which Jacob (later named Israel) could only dream. This divine manifestation will be seen in the seven ensuing "signs" of the gospel and finally at the cross, the revelation of God's glory in Jesus Christ.

Reflection and Discussion

• What is the significance of the fact that nearly everyone who comes to Jesus does so on the basis of someone else's witness? Am I willing, like Andrew and Philip, to bring others to Jesus?

• What am I looking for? Am I willing to accept the invitation of Jesus to find out? How can I accept the invitation of Jesus to "come and see"?

• What obstacle is preventing me from experiencing a fuller and deeper life of discipleship? How would I like God to reveal himself to me?

• In what way does the image of Jacob's ladder express Jesus as the revelation of God?

Prayer

King of Israel, though people longed for your coming for centuries, you invite each person by name to come and experience your life. Thank you for linking heaven and earth and leading me to a deeper relationship with God and a fuller life in you.

"Everyone serves the good wine first, and then the inferior wine after the guests have become drunk. But you have kept the good wine until now."

John 2:10

Jesus Gives Abundant Wine for the Wedding Feast

JOHN 2:1–12 ¹*On the third day there was a wedding in Cana of Galilee, and the mother of Jesus was there.* ²*Jesus and his disciples had also been invited to the wedding.* ³*When the wine gave out, the mother of Jesus said to him, "They have no wine."* ⁴*And Jesus said to her, "Woman, what concern is that to you and to me? My hour has not yet come."* ⁵*His mother said to the servants, "Do whatever he tells you."* ⁶*Now standing there were six stone water jars for the Jewish rites of purification, each holding twenty or thirty gallons.* ⁷*Jesus said to them, "Fill the jars with water." And they filled them up to the brim.* ⁸*He said to them, "Now draw some out, and take it to the chief steward." So they took it.* ⁹*When the steward tasted the water that had become wine, and did not know where it came from (though the servants who had drawn the water knew), the steward called the bridegroom* ¹⁰*and said to him, "Everyone serves the good wine first, and then the inferior wine after the guests have become drunk. But you have kept the good wine until now."* ¹¹*Jesus did this, the first of his signs, in Cana of Galilee, and revealed his glory; and his disciples believed in him.*

¹²*After this he went down to Capernaum with his mother, his brothers, and his disciples; and they remained there a few days.*

Having gathered his disciples, Jesus brings them to a wedding feast in the town of Cana. Their invitation to come and see begins to take shape as they realize that following Jesus would mean their lives would never be the same again. Never again would life be as predictable, bland, and colorless as water; life in Jesus becomes vibrant, luscious, and effervescent. Jesus is the bringer of messianic joy. He has come to show people the life they have been missing.

Jesus' actions at the feast are described as "the first of his signs" by which he would reveal his glory (verse 11). The sign points beyond the event to the truth about who Jesus is. The miracle of the delicious wine is the first means of revealing the Father at work in Jesus, manifesting God's power and love, drawing people to his abundant life.

The site of the wedding feast is the small village of Cana, near Jesus' hometown of Nazareth. The mother of Jesus is the first of the wedding guests listed in the account. She is the one who informs Jesus, "They have no wine" (verse 3). Jesus' rebuke of his mother, "My hour has not yet come" (verse 4), indicates that this sign cannot be understood apart from that climactic "hour" of Jesus' death on the cross when the Father will be fully glorified in his Son. The glory manifested in this first sign and in Jesus' death must be understood together. The gift of wine is a prelude to the gift of his own life. The mother who was with Jesus at the beginning of his ministry will also return to the narrative at the end, his hour of glorification at the cross.

Meanwhile, the mother of Jesus facilitates the miracle by instructing the servants, "Do whatever he tells you" (verse 5). She models the type of confident trust that is the necessary precondition for the work of her son. In response, Jesus finds a way to meet the needs of the hour by performing an unobtrusive miracle. Only Jesus' mother, the chief steward, a few servants, and Jesus' disciples knew what happened. There is no indication that the other guests realized what Jesus had done. By acting discreetly, Jesus saves the host from any embarrassment and avoids stealing the spotlight from the wedding.

In Judaism wine is an expression of joyful celebration. The prophets of Israel had used images of abundant and quality wine to express the restoration of David's rule and the coming of the Messiah: "The mountains shall drip sweet wine, and all the hills shall flow with it" (Amos 9:13), and "The Lord of hosts will make for all peoples a feast of rich food, a feast of well-matured wines" (Isa 25:6). In this first sign, the emphasis is not only on the quantity of wine that filled the six stone jars to the top, but also on the quality of the wine. When the chief steward tasted it, he told the bridegroom, "You have kept the good wine until now" (verse 11). For those who trustingly follow Jesus and believe in him, life becomes an anticipation of the joyous wedding feast foretold by the prophets about the age to come.

Reflection and Discussion

• What could be some of the reasons why the evangelist chose this miracle at Cana as the first sign to reveal the glory of Jesus?

• The fact that the mother of Jesus is the first guest mentioned and the initiator of the miracle indicates that her role is crucial to the narrative. In what way does this account portray Mary as a model for Jesus' disciples?

• Am I trusting enough to do whatever Jesus tells me? How is my ordinary life transformed because of Jesus?

Prayer

Lord of the age to come, you turn water to wine and transform ordinary existence into abundant living. Manifest your power in my life today, and let me see God's presence in all the signs around me.

"This temple has been under construction for forty-six years, and will you raise it up in three days?" John 2:20

Jesus Clears the Temple in Preparation for Passover

JOHN 2:13–25 [13]*The Passover of the Jews was near, and Jesus went up to Jerusalem.* [14]*In the temple he found people selling cattle, sheep, and doves, and the money changers seated at their tables.* [15]*Making a whip of cords, he drove all of them out of the temple, both the sheep and the cattle. He also poured out the coins of the money changers and overturned their tables.* [16]*He told those who were selling the doves, "Take these things out of here! Stop making my Father's house a marketplace!"* [17]*His disciples remembered that it was written, "Zeal for your house will consume me."* [18]*The Jews then said to him, "What sign can you show us for doing this?"* [19]*Jesus answered them, "Destroy this temple, and in three days I will raise it up."* [20]*The Jews then said, "This temple has been under construction for forty-six years, and will you raise it up in three days?"* [21]*But he was speaking of the temple of his body.* [22]*After he was raised from the dead, his disciples remembered that he had said this; and they believed the scripture and the word that Jesus had spoken.*

[23]*When he was in Jerusalem during the Passover festival, many believed in his name because they saw the signs that he was doing.* [24]*But Jesus on his part would*

not entrust himself to them, because he knew all people ²⁵*and needed no one to testify about anyone; for he himself knew what was in everyone.*

L ike the other occurrences in John's gospel, the cleansing of the temple is, at a deeper level, a manifestation of the identity of Jesus. The reference to the feast of Passover makes this the first in a series of references to Jewish festivals, the cumulative effect of which is to present Jesus as the fulfillment of symbolism inherent in the various feasts and institutions of Judaism. The gospel demonstrates how all the aspects of Jewish worship point to Jesus and that, as Israel's Messiah, he embodies and completes them. First, Jesus shows how the temple system is corrupt and in dire need of reform and renewal. Then, Jesus reveals that he himself will become the true temple by passing through temporary destruction and being raised again on the third day (verse 19).

Jesus acts as the messianic prophet. He authoritatively enters the area of the temple and performs a prophetic action. He symbolically acts out God's impending judgment on the Jerusalem temple and signifies its coming destruction. His aggressive action expresses a challenge to the religious institution and its leadership that has grown too rigid and corrupt to express the new manifestation of God's presence in Christ.

After the resurrection of Jesus, his disciples "remembered" and "believed" both "the Scripture and the word Jesus had spoken" about the Temple (verse 22). The Scripture was Psalm 69:9, "Zeal for your house consumes me" (verse 17), and the words Jesus had spoken were "Destroy this temple, and in three days I will raise it up" (verse 19). The significance of these words became clear to the disciples only after the death and resurrection of Jesus (verse 21). Jesus was indeed consumed, even to the point of death, by his zeal for God's house, for the presence of God in the world. But the divine presence did not require the physical temple of Jerusalem, for the Word had become flesh in the world. The temple that would be destroyed and rebuilt in three days was Jesus himself, the new means of access to the unseen God, the new "temple" for the messianic age.

If, as seems probable, John wrote his gospel after the obliteration of the Jerusalem temple in AD 70 by the Romans, we can assume that the devastation of that destruction was a major motivation for writing the gospel. As the

Jewish people were left without a sanctuary where they could come into God's presence and worship, John wanted to demonstrate how Jesus himself was the new temple that replaced the old. As Jesus drove out the sheep, cattle, and doves used for sacrifice, he foreshadowed the permanent cessation of sacrificial worship in the temple and its replacement by his own death. The glory of God, which had filled the temple of old, would be manifested, not in a building, but in the person of God's Messiah. As the temple had been the unifying symbol for God's people, the crucified and risen body of Christ would be the eternal sanctuary, uniting both Jews and Gentiles in the everlasting worship of God.

Reflection and Discussion

• Why are religious institutions so easily corrupted? What needs to be expelled from the church so that it can better express the presence of God?

• What are some of the ways that John's gospel presents Jesus himself as the new temple?

Prayer

Lord Jesus, you are the new temple which was destroyed and raised up forever. Accept the sacrifice of my life, and unite it with your death and resurrection to become a perfect offering to the Father.

SUGGESTIONS FOR FACILITATORS, GROUP SESSION 2

1. If there are newcomers who were not present for the first group session, introduce them now.

2. You may want to pray this prayer as a group:

Creator God, we worship Jesus as the Word of God, the Lamb of God, Son of God, the Messiah, and King of Israel. Jesus gradually disclosed his full identity to the people of the gospel, and he reveals himself to us through these inspired words. Give us a deep desire to know Jesus more completely, and call us to live a fuller life in him. Manifest the presence of the Word Made Flesh among us today, and help us discern his divine presence in all the signs around us. As we study, reflect, and pray with the Gospel of John, send us your Spirit to guide and direct us.

3. Ask one or more of the following questions:
- What was your biggest challenge in Bible study over this past week?
- What did you learn about yourself this week?

4. Discuss lessons 1 through 6 together. Assuming that group members have read the Scripture and commentary during the week, there is no need to read it aloud. As you review each lesson, you might want to briefly summarize the Scripture passages of each lesson and ask the group what stands out most clearly from the commentary.

5. Choose one or more of the questions for reflection and discussion from each lesson to talk over as a group. You may want to ask group members which question was most challenging or helpful to them as you review each lesson.

6. Keep the discussion moving, but don't rush the discussion in order to complete more questions. Allow time for the questions that provoke the most discussion.

7. Instruct group members to complete lessons 7 through 12 on their own during the six days before the next group meeting. They should write out their own answers to the questions as preparation for next week's group discussion.

8. Conclude by praying aloud together the prayer at the end of lesson 6, or any other prayer you choose.

"Very truly, I tell you, no one can see the kingdom of God
without being born from above." John 3:3

Nicodemus Comes to the Light

JOHN 3:1–21 ¹*Now there was a Pharisee named Nicodemus, a leader of the Jews. ²He came to Jesus by night and said to him, "Rabbi, we know that you are a teacher who has come from God; for no one can do these signs that you do apart from the presence of God." ³Jesus answered him, "Very truly, I tell you, no one can see the kingdom of God without being born from above." ⁴Nicodemus said to him, "How can anyone be born after having grown old? Can one enter a second time into the mother's womb and be born?" ⁵Jesus answered, "Very truly, I tell you, no one can enter the kingdom of God without being born of water and Spirit. ⁶What is born of the flesh is flesh, and what is born of the Spirit is spirit. ⁷Do not be astonished that I said to you, 'You must be born from above.' ⁸The wind blows where it chooses, and you hear the sound of it, but you do not know where it comes from or where it goes. So it is with everyone who is born of the Spirit." ⁹Nicodemus said to him, "How can these things be?" ¹⁰Jesus answered him, "Are you a teacher of Israel, and yet you do not understand these things?*

¹¹*"Very truly, I tell you, we speak of what we know and testify to what we have seen; yet you do not receive our testimony. ¹²If I have told you about earthly things and you do not believe, how can you believe if I tell you about heavenly things? ¹³No one has ascended into heaven except the one who descended from*

heaven, the Son of Man. ¹⁴*And just as Moses lifted up the serpent in the wilderness, so must the Son of Man be lifted up,* ¹⁵*that whoever believes in him may have eternal life.*

¹⁶*"For God so loved the world that he gave his only Son, so that everyone who believes in him may not perish but may have eternal life.*

¹⁷*"Indeed, God did not send the Son into the world to condemn the world, but in order that the world might be saved through him.* ¹⁸*Those who believe in him are not condemned; but those who do not believe are condemned already, because they have not believed in the name of the only Son of God.* ¹⁹*And this is the judgment, that the light has come into the world, and people loved darkness rather than light because their deeds were evil.* ²⁰*For all who do evil hate the light and do not come to the light, so that their deeds may not be exposed.* ²¹*But those who do what is true come to the light, so that it may be clearly seen that their deeds have been done in God."*

Nicodemus is identified as both a Pharisee and "a leader of the Jews" (verse 1). He was most probably a member in Jerusalem of the Sanhedrin, the national council in charge of Jewish affairs. He represents those Jewish leaders who come to know that Jesus is "a teacher who has come from God" because of the "signs" he performs (verse 2). His approach to Jesus "by night" seemingly indicates that he does not want other Pharisees to know about his interest in Jesus. But at a deeper level it means that he is leaving the darkness in order to come to Jesus, "the light that has come into the world" (verse 19).

Though Nicodemus has been attracted to Jesus through his teachings and signs, Jesus immediately states the foundation of the new life he offers. Experiencing the kingdom of God requires nothing less than a spiritual regeneration, a new birth (verses 3, 7). The Greek adverb that describes this new birth, *anothen*, means both "again" and "from above." The new era in humanity's relationship with God requires a life that is radically new: one must be born again/from above.

Nicodemus can only understand the physical meaning of Jesus' words and naively inquires how an older person can enter the womb again and be born (verse 4). Jesus further develops his teaching and explains that one must be "born of water and Spirit" (verse 5). New birth, expressed in Christian baptism, means embracing the fullness of life that God wants to give. Using the Greek word *pneuma*, which means both "spirit" and "wind," Jesus explains that the process and results of this new birth are as mysterious as the wind, far beyond human understanding or control.

When Nicodemus inquires of Jesus, "How can these things be?" Jesus responds that the new and eternal life can only be given when people "believe" (verses 12, 14, 16, 18). Jesus offers an analogy by recalling how God told Moses in the wilderness to mount a bronze serpent on a pole as a way of healing his people (Num 21:8–9). The Israelites looked up at the serpent in order to be restored to life; the one who believes in Jesus lifted up on the cross receives eternal life (verse 15). The process of believing does not mean simply accepting the facts of Jesus' teachings and signs, but personally receiving and surrendering to the full implications of God's saving love.

Unlike God's saving deeds with Israel in the past, the scope of God's saving love is worldwide: "God so loved the world that he gave his only Son" (verse 16). God did not send his Son to condemn the world, but "so that the world might be saved through him" (verse 17). But the reason people do not accept God's love and "believe in him" is because of their love for darkness and fear that their evil deeds will be exposed in the light (verses 19–20). When people discover the light, they are faced with the choice of either coming into the light and recognizing their sins or running back into the darkness so as not to see their lives clearly. When people welcome the light and confess their sins, they do what is true and receive eternal light.

Reflection and Discussion

• In what direction does God's Spirit seem to be blowing today? What is the Spirit's effects on my life and that of Christ's church?

• Why is it necessary to be born from above if we are to experience the life God wishes to give us? Where am I in the birthing process?

• In what ways does the bronze serpent lifted up in the wilderness express the life-giving power of Jesus?

• "The light has come into the world." What is the choice that this reality presents for Nicodemus and for all who read the Gospel of John?

Prayer

Rabbi Jesus, help me to seek the light of your teachings and the saving love you offer to the world. Let your Spirit blow within me, motivating my desire for you and opening my life to the new birth of truth and lasting life.

"The friend of the bridegroom, who stands and hears him, rejoices greatly at the bridegroom's voice." John 3:30

He Must Increase, but I Must Decrease

JOHN 3:22–36 *²²After this Jesus and his disciples went into the Judean countryside, and he spent some time there with them and baptized. ²³John also was baptizing at Aenon near Salim because water was abundant there; and people kept coming and were being baptized ²⁴—John, of course, had not yet been thrown into prison.*

²⁵Now a discussion about purification arose between John's disciples and a Jew. ²⁶They came to John and said to him, "Rabbi, the one who was with you across the Jordan, to whom you testified, here he is baptizing, and all are going to him." ²⁷John answered, "No one can receive anything except what has been given from heaven. ²⁸You yourselves are my witnesses that I said, 'I am not the Messiah, but I have been sent ahead of him.' ²⁹He who has the bride is the bridegroom. The friend of the bridegroom, who stands and hears him, rejoices greatly at the bridegroom's voice. For this reason my joy has been fulfilled. ³⁰He must increase, but I must decrease."

³¹The one who comes from above is above all; the one who is of the earth belongs to the earth and speaks about earthly things. The one who comes from heaven is above all. ³²He testifies to what he has seen and heard, yet no one accepts his testimony. ³³Whoever has accepted his testimony has certified this, that God is true. ³⁴He whom God has sent speaks the words of God, for he gives the Spirit without measure. ³⁵The Father loves the Son and has placed all things in his hands. ³⁶Whoever believes in the Son has eternal life; whoever disobeys the Son will not see life, but must endure God's wrath.

John the Baptist, the first witness to the work of Jesus in the world, here appears for the last time in the gospel. We realize, only in this gospel, that there was a period in which the ministries of John and Jesus overlapped, both of them maintaining vibrant, attractive ministries. It seems that John and Jesus are now both baptizing, but in different locations (verses 22–23), though the gospel later indicates that Jesus himself was not baptizing but only his disciples (4:2). We sense a degree of jealousy as John's disciples express concern that Jesus is drawing people away from John (verse 26). But rather than defend his role, John states that what determines the respective roles of Jesus and John is "what has been given from heaven" (verse 27). God has decided the task of John, and he must not compare himself with others or exceed the call he has received.

John the Baptist declares that his role is like that of the best man at a wedding. He rejoices when the groom summons him to the festivities and stands ready to do the groom's bidding (verse 29). In view of the Old Testament texts in which Israel is the bride of God, John is here announcing that Jesus is the long-awaited Messiah. The transition from John to Jesus marks the defining moment of the history of salvation, the movement from the era of the prophets to that of the Messiah. John knows that his purpose has been to elevate Jesus: "He must increase, but I must decrease" (verse 30). With Jesus on the ascendancy, John knows it is time for his own work to come to a close.

The truth that "the Father loves the Son and has placed all things in his hands" (verse 35) is the foundation upon which the Gospel of John is constructed. Because of his intimacy with the Father, Jesus speaks the words of God (verse 34). He is the mouth of God in the world, speaking God's eternal truths in ways we can understand. God gave the Spirit to the prophets in measured amounts, but Jesus is the one on whom the Spirit has come to rest in all its fullness. Because of this boundless richness, he is the one who "gives the Spirit without measure." Jesus produces abundant wine, offers an abundance of the Spirit, and wants us to share life in abundance forever (verse 36; also 10:10).

Reflection and Discussion

• What can I learn from John the Baptist about being a witness to Jesus? What are my responsibilities and my limitations in Christian witness?

• What are the indicators in the gospel that Jesus offers us not only unending life but also abundant life? How do I experience the abundance that Jesus wants to give me?

• In interpreting John the Baptist's acknowledgment, "He must increase, but I must decrease," St. Augustine said, "I am in the place of hearer; he, of speaker; I am as one who must be enlightened, he is the light; I am the ear, he is the word." What challenge do the words of John offer me?

Prayer

Heavenly Bridegroom, I rejoice that you have invited me to share in the abundant wine, joy, and spirit of your wedding feast. Encourage me to accept your invitation and to live gratefully in your Holy Spirit.

"Everyone who drinks of this water will be thirsty again,
but those who drink of the water that I will give them will never be thirsty."
John 4:13–14

Jesus Offers Living Water to the Woman of Samaria

JOHN 4:1–15 ¹*Now when Jesus learned that the Pharisees had heard, "Jesus is making and baptizing more disciples than John"* ²*—although it was not Jesus himself but his disciples who baptized—*³*he left Judea and started back to Galilee.* ⁴*But he had to go through Samaria.* ⁵*So he came to a Samaritan city called Sychar, near the plot of ground that Jacob had given to his son Joseph.* ⁶*Jacob's well was there, and Jesus, tired out by his journey, was sitting by the well. It was about noon.*

⁷*A Samaritan woman came to draw water, and Jesus said to her, "Give me a drink."* ⁸*(His disciples had gone to the city to buy food.)* ⁹*The Samaritan woman said to him, "How is it that you, a Jew, ask a drink of me, a woman of Samaria?" (Jews do not share things in common with Samaritans.)* ¹⁰*Jesus answered her, "If you knew the gift of God, and who it is that is saying to you, 'Give me a drink,' you would have asked him, and he would have given you living water."* ¹¹*The woman said to him, "Sir, you have no bucket, and the well is deep. Where do you get that living water?* ¹²*Are you greater than our ancestor Jacob, who gave us the well, and with his sons and his flocks drank from it?"* ¹³*Jesus said to her, "Everyone who drinks of this water will be thirsty again,* ¹⁴*but those who drink*

39

of the water that I will give them will never be thirsty. The water that I will give will become in them a spring of water gushing up to eternal life." [15]*The woman said to him, "Sir, give me this water, so that I may never be thirsty or have to keep coming here to draw water."*

As Jesus left Judea and headed back to Galilee, the texts says, "He had to go through Samaria" (verse 4). This route was not a geographical necessity. In fact, Jews would often travel a longer, less direct route along the valley of the Jordan River, in order to avoid passing through Samaria. The people of Samaria were a people of mixed blood since their conquest by Assyria, and they maintained their own temple on Mount Gerizim, rather than worshiping God in the Jerusalem temple. The necessity that compelled Jesus to travel through Samaria is the divine necessity to move beyond the world of Judaism. This scene is the first hint that the gospel of salvation will eventually be extended beyond the people of Israel.

Presuming he and his disciples had begun their journey at daybreak, they had been traveling about six hours. Jesus was worn out from his journey; he was tired and thirsty. The Word become flesh involved a total divine condescension to the limitations and frailty of human nature. Yet, it is precisely this humility that opens up the way for the revelation of his true identity.

The well was the center of life for the ancient people of the Bible. It tapped into ground water, and so in the dry summers it was their source of life-sustaining water and their salvation from slow famine. It was also a gathering place, a place where people met for conversation and laughter. It was even a place where love began. It was at a well that Jacob met Rachel and Moses met Zipporah. So when Jesus meets the Samaritan woman at the well of Jacob, we should be prepared for an encounter filled with profound possibility.

The woman is shocked that Jesus should speak to her: "How is it that you, a Jew, ask a drink of me, a woman of Samaria?" (verse 9). A Jewish man of the time would ordinarily not speak to an unknown woman alone, and generally the Jews ignored—if not detested—the Samaritans. Jesus did not plead ignorance; he was fully aware of the social rules and the Jewish intolerance of Samaritans. Yet, Jesus frequently broke social and religious boundaries for a higher good. Here Jesus uses his physical thirst as the occasion to address the deeper thirst of the Samaritan woman.

Jesus responded that if the woman knew who he was, she would have asked him for a drink—and he would have given her not well water but "living water" (verse 10). On the natural level, living water is flowing water, the water of a spring that is always fresh and sparkling. But the real contrast is between the well water of ordinary existence and the living water of abundant life in God's Spirit (verses 13–14). The woman begins to realize that Jesus is offering her far more than water. The repeated emphasis on being "thirsty" indicates that Jesus is ministering to a need that is experienced intensely. The "spring of water gushing up to eternal life" that Jesus offers recalls Isaiah's vision of the last days when people will joyfully "draw water from the wells of salvation" (Isa 12:3). Though the woman clearly desires the water that Jesus has to offer, she is still at a loss to understand its origin. Jesus wants to bestow upon her a new kind of life, a life that begins with forgiveness and baptism and then extends into eternal life.

Reflection and Discussion

• Jesus frequently crossed boundaries that divided people, in order to show that God's grace is available to all people. What does Jesus' encounter with the Samaritan woman teach me about God's favor and work in the world?

• What are the barriers that I erect between myself and other people? What boundaries do I need to cross today in order to live up to my Christian mission?

• What is significant about the fact that Jesus encounters the Samaritan woman at a well?

• The experience of thirst penetrates this passage: the thirst of Jesus, the thirst of the woman, and the thirst of the world. When have I been thirsty, physically or spiritually? In what way does "living water" express the kind of life that Jesus gives to me? How thirsty am I for the living waters that Jesus offers me?

• In what way is "living water" a symbol of the kind of life Jesus offers us?

Prayer

Source of living water, help me to realize my thirsts for you and for the new life you offer me. Quench my thirst with the gift of your Spirit, and renew the grace of baptism within me.

"The hour is coming, and is now here, when the true worshipers will worship the Father in spirit and truth." John 4:23

The Samaritan Woman Leaves Her Water Jar Behind

JOHN 4:16–30 ¹⁶*Jesus said to her, "Go, call your husband, and come back."* ¹⁷*The woman answered him, "I have no husband." Jesus said to her, "You are right in saying, 'I have no husband';* ¹⁸*for you have had five husbands, and the one you have now is not your husband. What you have said is true!"* ¹⁹*The woman said to him, "Sir, I see that you are a prophet.* ²⁰*Our ancestors worshiped on this mountain, but you say that the place where people must worship is in Jerusalem."* ²¹*Jesus said to her, "Woman, believe me, the hour is coming when you will worship the Father neither on this mountain nor in Jerusalem.* ²²*You worship what you do not know; we worship what we know, for salvation is from the Jews.* ²³*But the hour is coming, and is now here, when the true worshipers will worship the Father in spirit and truth, for the Father seeks such as these to worship him.* ²⁴*God is spirit, and those who worship him must worship in spirit and truth."* ²⁵*The woman said to him, "I know that Messiah is coming" (who is called Christ). "When he comes, he will proclaim all things to us."* ²⁶*Jesus said to her, "I am he, the one who is speaking to you."*

²⁷*Just then his disciples came. They were astonished that he was speaking with a woman, but no one said, "What do you want?" or, "Why are you speaking with her?"* ²⁸*Then the woman left her water jar and went back to the city. She said to the*

people, ²⁹*"Come and see a man who told me everything I have ever done! He cannot be the Messiah, can he?"* ³⁰*They left the city and were on their way to him.*

The prophetic insight of Jesus about the Samaritan woman's marital state is usually interpreted as his attempt to get the woman to acknowledge her sinful past in order to receive the new life he is offering her. The woman admits that she has no husband, and Jesus acknowledges that she is correct, for she has had five husbands, and the one with her now is not her husband (verses 17–18). While this quite possibly recounts a tragic marital history, there is an ancient interpretation of this text that is quite attractive. The book of Second Kings describes the resettlement of Samaria after the Assyrian conquest. People from five foreign nations settled there and mixed with the remaining people of Israel. Each of these peoples brought their own gods and religious practices, which compromised the covenant faith of Israel (2 Kings 17:24, 29–34). If the five husbands of the Samaritan woman symbolize Samaria's relationships with these five idolatrous peoples, then the sixth, or present liaison, would be Samaria's infidelity to God by their worship on Mount Gerizim rather than Jerusalem.

This interpretation seems more probable in light of the Samaritan woman's response to Jesus, which has nothing to do with marriage, but is concerned with the correct place for worshiping God. The Samaritans considered Mount Gerizim the proper place of sacrifice, while Jews held for Jerusalem as the only suitable place (verse 20). Jesus replies that the place of worship will be relatively unimportant in the new relationship with God that he offers. The new temple for all people will be the body of the risen Lord (2:19–21), in which people will worship in spirit and truth (verse 24).

As the woman departs from the well to tell the good news in the city, she leaves behind her water jar (verse 28). The gospel writer's mention of the abandoned water jar is an intriguing detail. Perhaps it expresses the fact that she now possesses living water and will never thirst again (verse 14). Perhaps it conveys her haste and apostolic zeal to witness to Jesus. Most interestingly, many commentators see it as the feminine counterpart to the male disciples leaving behind their nets and boats to follow Jesus.

The Samaritan woman's style of evangelizing can be a refreshing model for our own. She has no certain answers, no prepackaged formulas she tries to impose on her listeners. Her witness is invitational. She encourages others to "come and see" what she herself has experienced in Jesus (verse 29). Her faith is still tentative and undeveloped. She is still full of questions: "He cannot be the Messiah, can he?" She invites others to share in her searching. Though her belief is still hesitant and immature, she demonstrates an apostolic zeal, since it is impossible to keep such good news to oneself.

Reflection and Discussion

• Was Jesus speaking about the Samaritan woman's marital history or the religious history of her people? Could he be speaking of both?

• What does the woman's leaving behind her water jar indicate about Jesus' impact on her? What kind of an impact does she have on others?

• Are the objects of my affection compatible with my faith in God? What idols distract my worship in spirit and truth? How might God want to renew my worship?

Prayer

Lord Jesus, you are the Messiah of Israel and the new temple for all people to worship the Father. Take away from me all that diverts my attention from genuine worship. May I always seek your truth and praise you in the Spirit.

"It is no longer because of what you said
that we believe, for we have heard for ourselves, and we know that
this is truly the Savior of the world." John 4:42

The Samaritans Come to Jesus

JOHN 4:31–42 ³¹*Meanwhile the disciples were urging him, "Rabbi, eat something." ³²But he said to them, "I have food to eat that you do not know about." ³³So the disciples said to one another, "Surely no one has brought him something to eat?" ³⁴Jesus said to them, "My food is to do the will of him who sent me and to complete his work. ³⁵Do you not say, 'Four months more, then comes the harvest'? But I tell you, look around you, and see how the fields are ripe for harvesting. ³⁶The reaper is already receiving wages and is gathering fruit for eternal life, so that sower and reaper may rejoice together. ³⁷For here the saying holds true, 'One sows and another reaps.' ³⁸I sent you to reap that for which you did not labor. Others have labored, and you have entered into their labor."*

³⁹*Many Samaritans from that city believed in him because of the woman's testimony, "He told me everything I have ever done." ⁴⁰So when the Samaritans came to him, they asked him to stay with them; and he stayed there two days. ⁴¹And many more believed because of his word. ⁴²They said to the woman, "It is no longer because of what you said that we believe, for we have heard for ourselves, and we know that this is truly the Savior of the world."*

The disciples have returned to Jesus, and the Samaritan woman has returned to her city. The contrast between the male disciples and the woman could not be greater. While the men are "astonished that he was speaking with a woman" (verse 27), this astonishing woman has gone forth to witness to Jesus (verses 28–29). While the men are occupied with eating the food they had bought, the woman was evangelizing the Samaritans. While the disciples are trying to understand why Jesus doesn't seem hungry (verses 31–33), the Samaritans were already leaving their city to come to Jesus as a result of the woman's testimony (verse 30). Clearly this woman does the work of an apostle: proclaiming the good news, witnessing to Jesus, and bringing others to him.

As the disciples are urging Jesus to eat something, Jesus states that he is sustained and nourished by doing the work of the Father: "My food is to do the will of him who sent me and to complete his work" (verse 34). Likewise, the "daily bread" of us who follow Jesus must be seeking God's will and carrying out the work he has given us. Even though we might maintain a balanced diet of physical food, we become malnourished unless we are sustained by a meaningful life in relationship to God. Jesus invites his disciples to the nourishing work of reaping the harvest that will result from what Jesus is sowing. Jesus tells them to look around and see the Samaritans coming to faith in him, like fields ripe for harvesting (verse 35). Jesus, sent by the Father (verse 34), in turn sends his disciples to continue his work (verse 38).

The Samaritan woman becomes an effective witness to Jesus, as she goes out to tell her villagers what she has experienced (verse 39). She demonstrates a zeal like Jesus', since it is impossible to keep such good news to oneself. Her faith in Jesus continually deepens through her encounter with him: she has come to believe first that Jesus is a prophet (verse 19), then the Messiah (verses 25–26), and finally, along with increasingly more Samaritans, Savior of the world (verse 42). Though the Samaritans must have seemed to the Jews of the time unlikely prospects for salvation, the seeds of grace are sown in unlikely places and reap fruit for eternal life (verse 36). Many Samaritans came to believe in Jesus "because of the woman's testimony" (verse 39). Then, when they welcomed Jesus into their lives and spent time with him, "many more believed because of his word" (verse 41). They came to know and trust for themselves that Jesus is "truly the Savior of the world." God's purposes are being fulfilled: God sent his Son into the world "in order that the world might be saved through him" (3:17).

Reflection and Discussion

• What nourishes and sustains my life? What is the "daily bread" for which I pray? What is the fruit I am called to reap for God in the world?

• The Samaritan woman is the most effective evangelizer in the whole gospel. What does she have to teach disciples about witness and missionary endeavors?

• What new insights have emerged from my engagement with the story of the Samaritan woman?

Prayer

Savior of the world, I thank you for sowing the seed of your word within me through the labor of others before me. As my life ripens for the harvest, you invite me to the mission of sowing your life in the hearts of others. May I rejoice with you when others come to believe in you.

When he heard that Jesus had come from Judea to Galilee, he went and begged him to come down and heal his son, for he was at the point of death. John 4:47

Jesus Heals the Royal Official's Son

JOHN 4:43–54 ⁴³*When the two days were over, he went from that place to Galilee* ⁴⁴*(for Jesus himself had testified that a prophet has no honor in the prophet's own country).* ⁴⁵*When he came to Galilee, the Galileans welcomed him, since they had seen all that he had done in Jerusalem at the festival; for they too had gone to the festival.*

⁴⁶*Then he came again to Cana in Galilee where he had changed the water into wine. Now there was a royal official whose son lay ill in Capernaum.* ⁴⁷*When he heard that Jesus had come from Judea to Galilee, he went and begged him to come down and heal his son, for he was at the point of death.* ⁴⁸*Then Jesus said to him, "Unless you see signs and wonders you will not believe."* ⁴⁹*The official said to him, "Sir, come down before my little boy dies."* ⁵⁰*Jesus said to him, "Go; your son will live." The man believed the word that Jesus spoke to him and started on his way.* ⁵¹*As he was going down, his slaves met him and told him that his child was alive.* ⁵²*So he asked them the hour when he began to recover, and they said to him, "Yesterday at one in the afternoon the fever left him."* ⁵³*The father realized that this was the hour when Jesus had said to him, "Your son will live." So he himself believed, along with his*

whole household. ⁵⁴*Now this was the second sign that Jesus did after coming from Judea to Galilee.*

J esus has traveled from Judea, through Samaria, and returned back to Galilee. He is welcomed by people who had seen the things he had done in Jerusalem, for they too had made the pilgrimage to the city for the festival of Passover (verse 45). The Galileans are in the same class as the people of Jerusalem who had challenged Jesus to prove his authority by working a miracle (2:18) and who had come to believe based on the signs he worked (2:23). The account that unfolds, however, is based on the faith of a Galilean who did not fit this class of miracle-seekers.

The royal official, whose son was sick some distance away in Capernaum, made the uphill journey all the way to Cana after hearing that Jesus was there. He pleads with Jesus to heal his dying son (verse 47). Despite Jesus' critique of those who seek signs and wonders, the man persists in his request (verse 48–49). The heart of the account comes when Jesus assures the man that his son will live and the man "believed the word that Jesus spoke to him" (verse 50). This is an effective faith, a belief based not on signs and wonders, but on the word of Jesus.

The official's son is healed by Jesus from afar, not by his touch but by his spoken word. Unlike other Galileans, the man takes Jesus at his word and departs. As the man journeys home to Capernaum, he is met by his slaves who told him that his son was alive, and that the fever had left him at about one in the afternoon, the very hour that Jesus had told his father, "Your son will live." The faith of the royal official leads his whole household to faith (verse 53).

The healing of the official's son is described as "the second sign" Jesus performed. Clearly what is important about these signs is not their external content, the wonder of the miracle, but the meaning beneath the sign that enables the recipient to come to a deeper knowledge of Jesus. The official demonstrates a remarkable progression from one who seeks out Jesus based on his reputation as a wonder-worker, to one who trusts in Jesus' word without seeing a miracle or validating sign, to believing in Jesus along with his entire household.

Though it is not explicitly stated, this royal official is most probably a Gentile, a representative of the broader world beyond Judaism. If so, then Jesus' encounters with Nicodemus, the Samaritan woman, and the royal official express the pattern of the early church's mission. The Acts of the Apostles demonstrates that the church advanced from Jerusalem, to Judea and Samaria, to the ends of the earth (Acts 1:8). Jesus first encountered Nicodemus, the Jewish official (3:1–5), then the Samaritan woman (4:1–42), and finally, the Gentile official (4:46–54). Though Jesus clearly states that "salvation is from the Jews" (4:22), he increasingly moves outward, receiving an increasingly truer response of faith. Nicodemus comes to Jesus under the cover of darkness and does not positively witness to Jesus before his fellow members of the Sanhedrin. The Samaritan woman encounters Jesus in the noon brightness, gradually believes in Jesus, and becomes his witness to the whole village. The royal official also encounters Jesus at midday, believes in his word, and brings his entire household to faith in Jesus. This precedent from Jesus' mission served to validate the church's mission to the Samaritans and Gentiles, which had been underway already for several decades by the time John's gospel was written.

Reflection and Discussion

• What brought me to faith in Jesus? How does Jesus invite me to deepen my faith?

• What is the meaning of Jesus' rebuke of the Galileans, "Unless you see signs and wonders you will not believe" (verse 48)? What is the problem with a preoccupation with the miraculous?

• In what sense did the royal official demonstrate a deeper faith in Jesus than most of the Galileans?

• How does the gospel contrast Jesus' encounter with Nicodemus with that of the royal official? What does the contrast teach me about genuine belief in Jesus?

• How does Jesus' encounter with the Samaritan woman and the royal official validate the missionary outreach of the early church?

Prayer

Lord Jesus, give me a faith that goes beyond miraculous content and visible results. Heal my lack of belief, and preserve my faith through times of testing. Help me to know that you are truly the Savior of the world.

SUGGESTIONS FOR FACILITATORS, GROUP SESSION 3

1. Welcome group members and ask if there are any announcements anyone would like to make.

2. You may want to pray this prayer as a group:

Father, you reveal your Son to us as the heavenly Bridegroom, the Source of living water, the Messiah of Israel, and the Savior of the world. Open our lives to new birth in your Spirit so that we may experience a renewed and abundant life. Give us a faith that goes beyond miracles and wonders, and help us to trust in your Son and believe in your word. As you continue sowing the seed of your word within us through our study of John's gospel, help us to sow your life in the hearts of one another so that we may bear a rich harvest for you.

3. Ask one or more of the following questions:
   • Which image from the lessons this week stands out most to you?
   • What is the most important lesson you learned through your study this week?

4. Discuss lessons 7 through 12. Choose one or more of the questions for reflection and discussion from each lesson to discuss as a group. You may want to ask group members which question was most challenging or helpful to them as you review each lesson.

5. Remember that there are no definitive answers for these discussion questions. The insights of group members will add to the understanding of all. None of these questions require an expert.

6. After talking about each lesson, instruct group members to complete lessons 13 through 18 on their own during the six days before the next group meeting. They should write out their own answers to the questions as preparation for next week's group discussion.

7. Ask the group if anyone is having any particular problems with the Bible study during the week. You may want to share advice and encouragement within the group.

8. Conclude by praying aloud together the prayer at the end of one of the lessons discussed. You may add to the prayer based on the sharing that has occurred in the group.

"Sir, I have no one to put me into the pool
when the water is stirred up; and while I am making my way,
someone else steps down ahead of me." John 5:7

Jesus Heals the Paralyzed Man at the Pool

JOHN 5:1–18 ¹*After this there was a festival of the Jews, and Jesus went up to Jerusalem. ²Now in Jerusalem by the Sheep Gate there is a pool, called in Hebrew Beth-zatha, which has five porticoes. ³In these lay many invalids—blind, lame, and paralyzed. ⁵One man was there who had been ill for thirty-eight years. ⁶When Jesus saw him lying there and knew that he had been there a long time, he said to him, "Do you want to be made well?" ⁷The sick man answered him, "Sir, I have no one to put me into the pool when the water is stirred up; and while I am making my way, someone else steps down ahead of me." ⁸Jesus said to him, "Stand up, take your mat and walk." ⁹At once the man was made well, and he took up his mat and began to walk.*

Now that day was a sabbath. ¹⁰So the Jews said to the man who had been cured, "It is the sabbath; it is not lawful for you to carry your mat." ¹¹But he answered them, "The man who made me well said to me, 'Take up your mat and walk.'" ¹²They asked him, "Who is the man who said to you, 'Take it up and walk'?" ¹³Now the man who had been healed did not know who it was, for Jesus had disappeared in the crowd that was there. ¹⁴Later Jesus found him in the temple and said to him, "See, you have been made well! Do not sin any more, so that nothing worse happens to you." ¹⁵The man went away and told the Jews that it was Jesus who had made him well. ¹⁶Therefore the Jews started persecuting Jesus, because he was doing such things on the sabbath. ¹⁷But Jesus answered them, "My Father is still working, and I also am working." ¹⁸For this reason the Jews were seeking all the more to kill him, because he was not only breaking the sabbath, but was also calling God his own Father, thereby making himself equal to God.

Though John's gospel is characterized by its spiritual aura and layers of symbolism, it is also quite detailed in its physical descriptions. The pool where this healing occurred was just north of the temple and was fed by an intermittent spring popularly believed to have healing qualities. Among the large number of sick and disabled who gathered at the pool, Jesus focused on a man who had been ill for 38 years (verse 5). The irony of the scene, however, is that Jesus bypassed the pool and its gushing spring, which had just been so carefully described, and heals the sick man with only his spoken word: "Stand up, take your mat and walk" (verse 8).

Having just been healed of a lifelong illness, the man is harassed by the religious authorities for carrying his mat, an activity forbidden of the Sabbath (verse 10). The healed man shifts the blame to the one who healed him. When they discover it was Jesus, they harassed him as well for healing on the Sabbath. When confronted, Jesus responds by referring to God's actions on the Sabbath in the work of creation. God did not actually stop working after six days, but began the work of sustaining and watching over the world. In this sense, God works on the Sabbath in the same way that Jesus is working: "My Father is still working, and I also am working" (verse 17). This phrase is the practical equivalent of the phrase in the other gospels: "The Son of Man is lord even of the Sabbath" (Mark 2:28). Rather than a code of restrictive practices, the Sabbath is a celebration of God's sovereignty as creator and redeemer.

The crucial issues of this "sign" are the proper observance of the Sabbath and a true understanding of who Jesus is. The tension mounts as the religious authorities accuse Jesus of breaking the Sabbath, calling God his Father, and "making himself equal to God" (verse 18). Ironically, they express a true understanding of Jesus. He is guilty of the charges yet completely innocent.

The conflict continues as Jesus reinterprets the Sabbath on the basis of his relationship with the God of Israel, his Father, while the authorities cannot see beyond their customary laws of the Sabbath and seek a way to put him to death.

This episode begins a new literary section of the gospel (John 5–10) which focuses on the Jewish feasts. The following festivals of Israel serve as the setting and symbolism for the narrated words and deeds of Jesus: Sabbath (John 5), Passover (John 6), Booths/Tabernacles (7:1—10:21), and Dedication/Hanukkah (10:22–42). As both the Jews of the synagogues and the Christians of John's churches struggled to know how to celebrate the feasts of salvation history after the destruction of the temple, John's gospel expresses the fact that all the biblical institutions of Israel's worship are completed in Jesus the Messiah. The saving presence of God, traditionally celebrated in the temple and at the feasts, could now be experienced in and through Jesus. The rich symbolism, tradition, and theology of the feasts are not abandoned or replaced; rather, these former gifts of the Torah are now completed and perfected in the gift of Israel's Messiah.

Reflection and Discussion

• Imaginatively enter the scene at the pool in Jerusalem. What are some of the things you see, hear, taste, smell, and feel?

• Why does John choose this healing of the paralytic man for the third "sign" of his gospel? In what way does John elevate this healing from simply a demonstration of Jesus' power, to one of the seven signs?

• What is my most persistent infirmity? Do I want to be well? How might the healing power of Jesus work in my affliction?

• How does Jesus demonstrate a fuller understanding of the Sabbath than that offered by the religious authorities in Jerusalem?

• Why does John choose to integrate the Jewish feasts into his description of the life and ministry of Jesus?

Prayer

Lord of the Sabbath, you are always at work with the Father, sustaining creation and redeeming the world. Work deeply within me, bringing your saving power to my illnesses and healing my pessimism and my spiritual paralysis.

"Very truly, I tell you, the hour is coming, and is now here, when the dead will hear the voice of the Son of God, and those who hear will live."

John 5:25

Receiving Eternal Life through the Son

JOHN 5:19–30 ¹⁹*Jesus said to them, "Very truly, I tell you, the Son can do nothing on his own, but only what he sees the Father doing; for whatever the Father does, the Son does likewise.* ²⁰*The Father loves the Son and shows him all that he himself is doing; and he will show him greater works than these, so that you will be astonished.* ²¹*Indeed, just as the Father raises the dead and gives them life, so also the Son gives life to whomever he wishes.* ²²*The Father judges no one but has given all judgment to the Son,* ²³*so that all may honor the Son just as they honor the Father. Anyone who does not honor the Son does not honor the Father who sent him.* ²⁴*Very truly, I tell you, anyone who hears my word and believes him who sent me has eternal life, and does not come under judgment, but has passed from death to life.*

²⁵*"Very truly, I tell you, the hour is coming, and is now here, when the dead will hear the voice of the Son of God, and those who hear will live.* ²⁶*For just as the Father has life in himself, so he has granted the Son also to have life in himself;* ²⁷*and he has given him authority to execute judgment, because he is the Son of Man.* ²⁸*Do not be astonished at this; for the hour is coming when all who are in their graves will hear his voice* ²⁹*and will come out—those who have done*

good, to the resurrection of life, and those who have done evil, to the resurrection of condemnation.

[30]*"I can do nothing on my own. As I hear, I judge; and my judgment is just, because I seek to do not my own will but the will of him who sent me.*

Jesus defends his authority to work on the Sabbath and his claim of equality with God. Breaking the Sabbath was a serious offense, but claiming oneself equal to God constituted blasphemy, the most serious offense of all. The encounter with the religious authorities shifts from dialogue to monologue.

Jesus explains his relationship with the Father by comparing their relationship to a human father and an apprenticed son. The son learns from the father through example and imitation. Referring to the relationship between the Father and the Son, Jesus says, "The Son can do nothing on his own, but only what he sees the Father doing" (verse 19). In all that Jesus does he is subject to the Father and dependent on the Father's power and love: "The Father loves the Son and shows him all that he himself is doing" (verse 20). Jesus asserts that although he is equal to God, he is functionally dependent on the Father and obedient to him. Rather than being independent of God, he is subordinate to him, as is a son to a father.

The "greater works" that the Father will show the Son, and that will "astonish" Jesus' accusers, involve the twin themes of life and judgment, both now and in the hereafter (verse 20). In the Old Testament, only the Lord of the Sabbath is the master of life and death, but because of the relationship between the Father and the Son, Jesus also carries out the work of giving eternal life and executing judgment (verses 21–29). The purpose of the Father's delegation of this authority to the Son is that people might honor the Son just as they honor the Father. Conversely, anyone who does not honor the Son also fails to honor the Father who sent him (verse 23).

These divine works of giving eternal life and rendering final judgment were understood within Judaism to be God's prerogative for the final age. But Jesus proclaims that these works of God, which were expected to happen in the future, were already happening in his own ministry. Eternal life is available now. Anyone who hears the word of Jesus and believes in the Father who sent him has crossed over to eternal life and is relieved of judgment and condemnation (verse 24). Through his ministry Jesus is giving life, the kind of life that lasts forever, and he is executing judgment, for as people accept or reject the revelation of God through him, they are even now condemned or vindicated.

Though the eternal life which Jesus proclaims is not just life after death but a quality of life that disciples can begin to experience here and now, the resurrection of the dead and the fullness of life will occur sometime in the future (verses 28–29). Those in the grave will hear the Messiah's voice and rise to the "resurrection of life" or to the "resurrection of condemnation." Notice that the division will take place on the basis of whether people have "done good" or "done evil." Belief often proves superficial, such as those who believe simply because they have seen signs and wonders. But believing the word of Jesus as God's revelation demands a changed life expressed in deeds and not merely words.

Reflection and Discussion

• In what sense can we say that the Son is equal with the Father? In what sense is Jesus also subordinate to the Father?

• How would I explain the words of Jesus in verse 24 to an inquirer seeking to understand the Christian way of life?

• What are the qualities of my present life that seem to be a sharing in eternal life? What parts of my present life would I want to last forever?

• In what sense can we say that God's judgment and eternal life are both present and future realities? In what ways do I experience judgment and eternal life in the present?

• What are the indicators that we are living in the final age?

Prayer

Lord of Life, you bestow your gift of eternal life upon those who believe in your word and live according to your teaching. Thank you for the gift of faith and discipleship. Help me to live abundantly today so that my present life is a foretaste of the life I will live eternally.

"You search the scriptures because you think that in them you have eternal life; and it is they that testify on my behalf." John 5:39

Jesus Calls His Witnesses to Give Testimony

JOHN 5:31–47 ³¹*"If I testify about myself, my testimony is not true.* ³²*There is another who testifies on my behalf, and I know that his testimony to me is true.* ³³*You sent messengers to John, and he testified to the truth.* ³⁴*Not that I accept such human testimony, but I say these things so that you may be saved.* ³⁵*He was a burning and shining lamp, and you were willing to rejoice for a while in his light.* ³⁶*But I have a testimony greater than John's. The works that the Father has given me to complete, the very works that I am doing, testify on my behalf that the Father has sent me.* ³⁷*And the Father who sent me has himself testified on my behalf. You have never heard his voice or seen his form,* ³⁸*and you do not have his word abiding in you, because you do not believe him whom he has sent.*

³⁹*"You search the scriptures because you think that in them you have eternal life; and it is they that testify on my behalf.* ⁴⁰*Yet you refuse to come to me to have life.* ⁴¹*I do not accept glory from human beings.* ⁴²*But I know that you do not have the love of God in you.* ⁴³*I have come in my Father's name, and you do not accept me; if another comes in his own name, you will accept him.* ⁴⁴*How can you believe when you accept glory from one another and do not seek the glory that comes from the one who alone is God?* ⁴⁵*Do not think that I will accuse you before the Father; your accuser is Moses, on whom you have set your hope.* ⁴⁶*If*

you believed Moses, you would believe me, for he wrote about me. [47]*But if you do not believe what he wrote, how will you believe what I say?"*

Jesus continues to defend himself before the religious authorities and speaks as if he were in a courtroom. He acknowledges that more than his own testimony is required for his defense (verse 31). The interrogation of witnesses was central to Jewish legal procedure, and at least two or three witnesses were necessary for a proceeding (Deut 17:6; 19:15). So Jesus begins calling his witnesses.

The first witness is John the Baptist, who has already testified to the truth about Jesus (verse 33). Jesus says John was "a burning and shining lamp" (verse 35), a reference to the psalm in which God said, "I have prepared a lamp for my anointed one" (Ps 132:17). John was that lamp, an important but temporary witness, that cast its light on the coming Messiah. The second witness is the testimony of Jesus' works (verse 36). The deeds that Jesus has been doing ought to testify to his divine origins. The third witness is the Father (verse 37). Yet the Father's voice cannot actually be heard and the Father's form cannot really be seen, except in Jesus himself. If they truly believed and his word abided in them, they would actually experience the Father in the person of Jesus. The final witness is Scripture (verse 39). The religious authorities search the Scriptures diligently in the hope of finding eternal life in them. Yet when the Scriptures point to Jesus as the way to life, the religious authorities are unwilling to come to him (verse 40).

Ultimately it is the Father who is the source of all these witnesses. He is the sender of John the Baptist. He is the one who empowers Jesus to perform his works. He sent Moses and inspired the Scriptures. In ancient times God revealed himself in salvation history, through Moses and the prophets. But in these last days, God reveals himself in his Son, through all his works.

Even though Jesus calls on the witnesses who testify to him, it becomes clear that the religious authorities are really the ones on trial. Jesus is not really the defendant but rather the prosecuting attorney. The Jewish leaders are on trial for their disbelief. Having so absorbed themselves in their religious duties and their own advancement, they have become spiritually blind and unable to perceive God's work in their midst. Their accuser is Moses (verse 45). If they believed Moses and the Scriptures that come from him, they would believe in

Jesus. The whole Torah and the prophets, the witness of the Old Testament, point to Jesus. The parallelism between what Moses wrote and what Jesus says, emphasizes the correspondence between the Hebrew Scriptures and the teachings of Jesus (verse 47). The unwillingness of the Jewish leaders to acknowledge the truth about Jesus calls into question their commitment to Scripture, the very heart of their faith and the basis of their hope.

Reflection and Discussion

• On what basis do I believe that Jesus is who the gospel claims him to be?

• Who are the credible witnesses that testify for me to the truth about Jesus? Am I a credible witness to Jesus?

• In what ways do the religious leaders in the gospel misunderstand and misuse the Scriptures? In what way do the Scriptures testify to Jesus?

Prayer

Giver of life and Judge of all, I entrust myself to you as my way to the Father and to eternal life. Help me to be a credible witness to you by the things I say and do each day.

"There is a boy here who has five barley loaves and two fish. But what are they among so many people?" John 6:9

Feeding the Multitude and Walking on Water

JOHN 6:1–21 *¹After this Jesus went to the other side of the Sea of Galilee, also called the Sea of Tiberias. ²A large crowd kept following him, because they saw the signs that he was doing for the sick. ³Jesus went up the mountain and sat down there with his disciples. ⁴Now the Passover, the festival of the Jews, was near. ⁵When he looked up and saw a large crowd coming toward him, Jesus said to Philip, "Where are we to buy bread for these people to eat?" ⁶He said this to test him, for he himself knew what he was going to do. ⁷Philip answered him, "Six months' wages would not buy enough bread for each of them to get a little." ⁸One of his disciples, Andrew, Simon Peter's brother, said to him, ⁹"There is a boy here who has five barley loaves and two fish. But what are they among so many people?" ¹⁰Jesus said, "Make the people sit down." Now there was a great deal of grass in the place; so they sat down, about five thousand in all. ¹¹Then Jesus took the loaves, and when he had given thanks, he distributed them to those who were seated; so also the fish, as much as they wanted. ¹²When they were satisfied, he told his disciples, "Gather up the fragments left over, so that nothing may be lost." ¹³So they gathered them up, and from the fragments of the five barley loaves, left by those who had eaten, they filled twelve baskets. ¹⁴When the people* *saw the sign that he had done, they began to say, "This is indeed the prophet who is to come into the world."*

15 When Jesus realized that they were about to come and take him by force to make him king, he withdrew again to the mountain by himself.

16 When evening came, his disciples went down to the sea, 17 got into a boat, and started across the sea to Capernaum. It was now dark, and Jesus had not yet come to them. 18 The sea became rough because a strong wind was blowing. 19 When they had rowed about three or four miles, they saw Jesus walking on the sea and coming near the boat, and they were terrified. 20 But he said to them, "It is I; do not be afraid." 21 Then they wanted to take him into the boat, and immediately the boat reached the land toward which they were going.

This chapter of the gospel follows the same pattern as the last chapter, in which Jesus' healing of the paralyzed man was followed by an extended discourse elaborating on the significance of the event. Here too, the wondrous signs of Jesus, feeding the multitude and walking on water, introduce the extensive discourse on the bread of life. Both chapters also elaborate on the significance of one of Judaism's institutions: the previous chapter on the Sabbath, and this one on the Passover festival.

The feast of Passover, celebrating the exodus from slavery, is the annual festival that most clearly expresses the identity of the people of Israel. Several elements of the exodus are brought to mind in the gospel text. Jesus' feeding of the five thousand (verse 11) recalls the feeding of the multitudes of Israelites with manna from God. Jesus' walking on water (verse 19) evokes the crossing of the sea during the Passover from bondage to freedom. The declaration of Jesus to his frightened disciples, "It is I. Do not be afraid" (verse 20), evokes the giving of the divine name to Moses and the Israelites.

John's gospel continually draws our attention to deeper levels of meaning in the actions of Jesus. What Jesus does reveals who he is. When the crowds see the "sign" that Jesus has done, they begin to proclaim him as the Messiah, "the prophet who is to come into the world" (verse 14). The crowds want to make him king so that they will have an unending supply of bread (verse 15). But Jesus is not only God's instrument (like Moses) in providing bread to sustain the life of his people, but he is himself sent by God as the life-giving bread who gives his life for the world. The miracle of the loaves and fish anticipates what

Jesus will do at the next Passover, when he will celebrate his last supper with his disciples and offer his life for their salvation.

Jesus' walking on the Sea of Galilee brings terror to his disciples. But Jesus is demonstrating God's mastery over the terrors of the sea and all the powers of storm and chaos in the world. In the midst of a violent storm that could wreak havoc on their wooden boat, the disciples see Jesus "walking on the sea," effortlessly coming toward them (verse 19). The greeting of Jesus, "It is I" assured the disciples that it was Jesus. But for the reader of the gospel, the Greek words *ego eimi* suggest far more. They are the words of the divine name, "I Am," the self-revelation of God in the Old Testament (Exod 3:14). The scene has a supernatural quality about it, and the presence of Jesus is elusive, offering the disciples a glimpse of the divine world. The scene alludes to Psalm 77, describing God's manifestation to Israel during the exodus and his faithful, redeeming love: "When the waters saw you, O God, when the waters saw you, they were afraid." While the clouds poured out rain, lightning lit up the sky, and thunder shook the earth, God made his way through the waters: "Your way was through the sea, your path, through the mighty waters; yet your footprints were unseen" (Ps 77:16–19). While the feeding of the loaves and fish revealed Jesus' messianic power to the multitudes, the walking on water is a private manifestation of his divine glory to his inner circle of disciples.

Reflection and Discussion

• What is the connection between these signs of Jesus and the coming feast of Passover?

• When have you experienced God stretching your limited resources and multiplying your own abilities far beyond what you could have imagined?

• In what way is Jesus' presence on the sea a divine manifestation?

• In what sense was Jesus testing Phillip when he saw the large crowd coming toward them? Can I trust in Jesus to satisfy my hungers and calm my fears?

Prayer

Master of the Sea, I often feel that I am overwhelmed by life's storms and the swirling chaos around me. Give me assurance that you can quiet the storms and tread the waters of the sea. Calm my fears and help me to trust you.

"I am the bread of life. Whoever comes to me will never be hungry, and whoever believes in me will never be thirsty." John 6:35

The Bread from Heaven Gives Life to the World

JOHN 6:22–51 *²²The next day the crowd that had stayed on the other side of the sea saw that there had been only one boat there. They also saw that Jesus had not got into the boat with his disciples, but that his disciples had gone away alone. ²³Then some boats from Tiberias came near the place where they had eaten the bread after the Lord had given thanks. ²⁴So when the crowd saw that neither Jesus nor his disciples were there, they themselves got into the boats and went to Capernaum looking for Jesus.*

²⁵When they found him on the other side of the sea, they said to him, "Rabbi, when did you come here?" ²⁶Jesus answered them, "Very truly, I tell you, you are looking for me, not because you saw signs, but because you ate your fill of the loaves. ²⁷Do not work for the food that perishes, but for the food that endures for eternal life, which the Son of Man will give you. For it is on him that God the Father has set his seal." ²⁸Then they said to him, "What must we do to perform the works of God?" ²⁹Jesus answered them, "This is the work of God, that you believe in him whom he has sent." ³⁰So they said to him, "What sign are you going to give us then, so that we may see it and believe you? What work are you performing? [31]Our ancestors ate the manna in the wilderness; as it is written, 'He gave them bread from heaven to eat.'" [32]Then Jesus said to them, "Very truly, I tell you, it was not Moses who gave you the bread from heaven, but it is my Father who gives you the true bread from heaven. [33]For the bread of God is that which comes down from heaven and gives life to the world." [34]They said to him, "Sir, give us this bread always."

[35]Jesus said to them, "I am the bread of life. Whoever comes to me will never be hungry, and whoever believes in me will never be thirsty. [36]But I said to you that you have seen me and yet do not believe. [37]Everything that the Father gives me will come to me, and anyone who comes to me I will never drive away; [38]for I have come down from heaven, not to do my own will, but the will of him who sent me. [39]And this is the will of him who sent me, that I should lose nothing of all that he has given me, but raise it up on the last day. [40]This is indeed the will of my Father, that all who see the Son and believe in him may have eternal life; and I will raise them up on the last day."

[41]Then the Jews began to complain about him because he said, "I am the bread that came down from heaven." [42]They were saying, "Is not this Jesus, the son of Joseph, whose father and mother we know? How can he now say, 'I have come down from heaven'?" [43]Jesus answered them, "Do not complain among yourselves. [44]No one can come to me unless drawn by the Father who sent me; and I will raise that person up on the last day. [45]It is written in the prophets, 'And they shall all be taught by God.' Everyone who has heard and learned from the Father comes to me. [46]Not that anyone has seen the Father except the one who is from God; he has seen the Father. [47]Very truly, I tell you, whoever believes has eternal life. [48]I am the bread of life. [49]Your ancestors ate the manna in the wilderness, and they died. [50]This is the bread that comes down from heaven, so that one may eat of it and not die. [51]I am the living bread that came down from heaven. Whoever eats of this bread will live forever; and the bread that I will give for the life of the world is my flesh."

The crowds who are searching for Jesus finally find him again on the other side of the lake. They do not understand how he got there, and Jesus perceives that they have come to him only because he gave them food. The underlying theme of this whole section will be the search for Jesus: how and why to seek him and where to find him. The crowd has been fed, but they have not yet begun to understand the significance of Jesus feeding them or what Jesus truly has to give (verses 25–26).

The crowd asked Jesus for a sign authenticating his authority so that they could see and believe, reminding Jesus that their ancestors had been given "bread from heaven to eat" (verses 30–31). Their emphasis that they "see" as the basis on which they "believe" represents inferior faith at best. Jesus explained that his Father was providing a far greater gift of food, bread from heaven that will give life to the whole world (verse 33). The true bread is not manna from the sky, but the flesh-and-blood person who stands before them. Jesus does not merely give bread from heaven; he is that bread. He is God's true sign, in all that he says and does.

Jesus proclaims the first of his seven "I Am" pronouncements, the proclamation of the ways Jesus brings us eternal life. "I am the bread of life" (verse 35). He is the food that never spoils, the bread that satisfies our deepest hunger. In contrast to material bread that perishes or even the "bread from heaven" given by God during the exodus, Jesus himself is the permanent food that gives everlasting life. The possession of "eternal life" is a present reality, and being raised on the last day is a future hope (verse 40). Because believers can trust that their future raising up by Jesus is a certainty, they already experience eternal life in the here and now. Believing in him means eternal life, now and forever (verse 47).

There are clear parallels between Jesus' Jewish opponents and the people of Israel during their wilderness journey (Exod 16:2, 8–9). Just as the Israelites complained about Moses, the first giver of heavenly bread, so now they complain about Jesus (verse 41). And just as in the journey of exodus, their complaining ultimately is directed against God himself. Jesus responded to them, "Do not complain among yourselves" (verse 43). He explains that no one can come to him unless drawn by the Father (verse 44). But when the Father draws them, people come to Jesus. There is a dynamic balance between God "drawing" and people "coming" to Jesus. When people allow themselves to be "taught by God" (verse 45) and receive God's revelation in Scripture, they will come to Jesus and believe in him. The reason why many refuse to come to him and believe is that they are unwilling to learn from God.

Jesus returns again and elaborates on his "I am" pronouncement (verse 48). There will be no death for the one who eats this bread (verse 50). Jesus himself is "the living bread that came down from heaven" (verse 51). He expresses the universal scope of his self-gift: "The bread that I will give for the life of the world is my flesh" (verse 51). The flesh of his body will be given over in sacrifice for the forgiveness of humanity's sins and for the life of the world.

Reflection and Discussion

• What are the similarities and differences between the manna in the wilderness and the "bread of life"?

• How does "I am the bread of life" indicate that Jesus is both the giver and the gift? What part is played by God and by the people in the process of coming to believe in Jesus?

• Do I hunger for what is temporary or for what is eternal? How do I feed the deepest hungers of my heart?

Prayer

Bread of Life, you were sent from heaven by the Father to feed the hearts of your hungry people. Help me to experience the satisfying nourishment of your presence, and give me the gift of eternal life.

"Those who eat my flesh and drink my blood have eternal life, and I will raise them up on the last day; for my flesh is true food and my blood is true drink." John 6:54–55

True Food and True Drink for Eternal Life

JOHN 6:52–71 *52 The Jews then disputed among themselves, saying, "How can this man give us his flesh to eat?" 53 So Jesus said to them, "Very truly, I tell you, unless you eat the flesh of the Son of Man and drink his blood, you have no life in you. 54 Those who eat my flesh and drink my blood have eternal life, and I will raise them up on the last day; 55 for my flesh is true food and my blood is true drink. 56 Those who eat my flesh and drink my blood abide in me, and I in them. 57 Just as the living Father sent me, and I live because of the Father, so whoever eats me will live because of me. 58 This is the bread that came down from heaven, not like that which your ancestors ate, and they died. But the one who eats this bread will live forever." 59 He said these things while he was teaching in the synagogue at Capernaum.*

60 When many of his disciples heard it, they said, "This teaching is difficult; who can accept it?" 61 But Jesus, being aware that his disciples were complaining about it, said to them, "Does this offend you? 62 Then what if you were to see the Son of Man ascending to where he was before? 63 It is the spirit that gives life; the flesh is useless. The words that I have spoken to you are spirit and life. 64 But among you there are some who do not believe." For Jesus knew from the first who were the ones that did not believe, and who was the one that would betray him. ⁶⁵*And he said, "For this reason I have told you that no one can come to me unless it is granted by the Father."*

⁶⁶*Because of this many of his disciples turned back and no longer went about with him.* ⁶⁷*So Jesus asked the twelve, "Do you also wish to go away?"* ⁶⁸*Simon Peter answered him, "Lord, to whom can we go? You have the words of eternal life.* ⁶⁹*We have come to believe and know that you are the Holy One of God."* ⁷⁰*Jesus answered them, "Did I not choose you, the twelve? Yet one of you is a devil."* ⁷¹*He was speaking of Judas son of Simon Iscariot, for he, though one of the twelve, was going to betray him.*

Four times in rapid succession Jesus speaks of the necessity of eating his flesh and drinking his blood (verses 53–56). The language of Jesus is shocking to his audience: eating his flesh literally implied cannibalism, and drinking blood was abhorrent to the Jewish mind (Lev 17:10–14). As is characteristic of the words of Jesus in John's Gospel, the sayings have multiple levels of meaning. The flesh and blood of Jesus is his very self. The result of a believer consuming his flesh and blood is mutual indwelling: "Those who eat my flesh and drink my blood abide in me, and I in them." To eat and drink of his very self is to participate fully in the mission and destiny of Jesus, in his life and his death. Eating his body and drinking his blood is to truly be his disciple—in following him, believing in him, and giving oneself with him for the life of the world. This is the nourishment that gives eternal life and victory over death (verses 51, 54, 58).

Undoubtedly, Jesus' words helped disciples understand the eucharistic sacrifice in the early church. Through the Eucharist, believers are invited to become one with Christ, as he and the Father are one, and through that intimate union, to experience eternal life (verse 57). Rather than connecting the Eucharist to the Last Supper as the final mandate of Jesus, as in the other gospels, John's gospel shows that the Eucharist flows from everything Jesus said and did as the Word Made Flesh. The Eucharist in this gospel is related not only to the death and resurrection of Jesus, but also to his incarnation. The Word Made Flesh gives his flesh as Eucharist, the sacramental climax of the mission of God's Word to the world.

Jesus contrasts the Old Testament banquet, in which Wisdom offers the invitation to "eat of my bread and drink of the wine" (Prov 9:5), with the banquet of his own flesh and blood. When people taste of Wisdom, they hunger and thirst for more (Sir 24:21), but Jesus, the Wisdom of God incarnate, offers a food that satisfies humanity's hunger and thirst completely.

After Jesus fed the hungry crowd, the people were ready to carry him away and make him king. But, as Jesus offered his discourse on the bread of life, the crowd moved from acclamation, to confusion, to hostility. Because this teaching of Jesus is difficult and demands a personal acceptance (verse 60), many of his disciples did not believe him (verse 64), and they left him and returned to their former way of life (verse 66). They decided that Jesus was not the Messiah they expected. Jesus then turns to this inner circle of disciples (called "the Twelve" for the first time in John's gospel): "Do you also wish to go away?" (verse 67). Peter's words are representative of the twelve. Because they have come to trust that Jesus is "the Holy One of God," they are able to accept his eucharistic teachings, with all their implications, as "the words of eternal life" (verses 68–69).

Ignatius, the early second century bishop of Antioch, seemed to understand the full meaning of Jesus' words. As he sailed toward Rome and his martyrdom, he wrote: "I want the bread of God, which is the flesh of Jesus Christ, and for drink I want his blood, which is incorruptible love." Ignatius knew that the Eucharist united him in the mission and destiny of Jesus, in his life and his death. Eating Christ's body and drinking his blood offers the nourishment that offers true life and victory over death.

Reflection and Discussion

• In what way does Jesus' eucharistic discourse focus on the real presence of Christ in the church's Eucharist? Which verse most convinces me that Jesus is really present in this gift of the Eucharist?

• As Jesus continued his discourse, the crowds moved from acclamation, to confusion, to hostility, and many of his disciples did not believe him and left him? Why were his words so difficult for so many?

• What does Jesus ask of me as I eat his body and drink his blood? Why is sharing in the Eucharist such a radical choice?

• The question of Jesus asked to the twelve is also asked of us all: "Do you also wish to go away?" What keeps me following Jesus through the challenges of discipleship?

Prayer

Lord of Life, you invite me to share deeply in your life by eating your flesh as true food and drinking your blood as true drink. Thank you for the gift of the Eucharist and for your gift of eternal life. Help me to remain in you, as you remain in me.

SUGGESTIONS FOR FACILITATORS, GROUP SESSION 4

1. Welcome group members and ask if anyone has any questions, announcements, or requests.

2. You may want to pray this prayer as a group:

God of all people, you give your gift of eternal life upon all who believe in your Son and live according to his teaching. Thank you for the gift of faith and discipleship. You sent your Son to feed the hearts of your hungry people. Help us to experience the satisfying nourishment of his presence as the Bread of Life. Help us to be credible witnesses to your Word Made Flesh by the things we say and do each day. Help us to live abundantly today so that our present lives are a foretaste of the life we will live forever.

3. Ask one or more of the following questions:
   - What is the most difficult part of this study for you?
   - What insights stand out to you from the lessons this week?

4. Discuss lessons 13 through 18. Choose one or more of the questions for reflection and discussion from each lesson to discuss as a group. You may want to ask group members which question was most challenging or helpful to them as you review each lesson.

5. Keep the discussion moving, but allow time for the questions that provoke the most discussion. Encourage the group members to use "I" language in their responses.

6. After talking over each lesson, instruct group members to complete lessons 19 through 24 on their own during the six days before the next group meeting. They should write out their own answers to the questions as preparation for next week's session.

7. Ask the group what encouragement they need for the coming week. Ask the members to pray for the needs of one another during the week.

8. Conclude by praying aloud together the prayer at the end of one of the lessons discussed. You may choose to conclude the prayer by asking members to pray aloud any requests they may have.

"Leave here and go to Judea so that your disciples also may see the works you are doing; for no one who wants to be widely known acts in secret." John 7:3–4

Pilgrimage to the Festival of Booths

JOHN 7:1–24 ¹*After this Jesus went about in Galilee. He did not wish to go about in Judea because the Jews were looking for an opportunity to kill him.* ²*Now the Jewish festival of Booths was near.* ³*So his brothers said to him, "Leave here and go to Judea so that your disciples also may see the works you are doing;* ⁴*for no one who wants to be widely known acts in secret. If you do these things, show yourself to the world."* ⁵*(For not even his brothers believed in him.)* ⁶*Jesus said to them, "My time has not yet come, but your time is always here.* ⁷*The world cannot hate you, but it hates me because I testify against it that its works are evil.* ⁸*Go to the festival yourselves. I am not going to this festival, for my time has not yet fully come."* ⁹*After saying this, he remained in Galilee.*

¹⁰*But after his brothers had gone to the festival, then he also went, not publicly but as it were in secret.* ¹¹*The Jews were looking for him at the festival and saying, "Where is he?"* ¹²*And there was considerable complaining about him among the crowds. While some were saying, "He is a good man," others were saying, "No, he is deceiving the crowd."* ¹³*Yet no one would speak openly about him for fear of the Jews.*

¹⁴*About the middle of the festival Jesus went up into the temple and began to*

teach. ¹⁵*The Jews were astonished at it, saying, "How does this man have such learning, when he has never been taught?"* ¹⁶*Then Jesus answered them, "My teaching is not mine but his who sent me.* ¹⁷*Anyone who resolves to do the will of God will know whether the teaching is from God or whether I am speaking on my own.* ¹⁸*Those who speak on their own seek their own glory; but the one who seeks the glory of him who sent him is true, and there is nothing false in him.*

¹⁹*"Did not Moses give you the law? Yet none of you keeps the law. Why are you looking for an opportunity to kill me?"* ²⁰*The crowd answered, "You have a demon! Who is trying to kill you?"* ²¹*Jesus answered them, "I performed one work, and all of you are astonished.* ²²*Moses gave you circumcision (it is, of course, not from Moses, but from the patriarchs), and you circumcise a man on the sabbath.* ²³*If a man receives circumcision on the sabbath in order that the law of Moses may not be broken, are you angry with me because I healed a man's whole body on the sabbath?* ²⁴*Do not judge by appearances, but judge with right judgment."*

The celebration of the feast of Booths, or Tabernacles, forms the setting and symbolism of this section of the gospel. The joyful festival celebrates the ingathering of the autumn fruit harvest and lasts for seven days. The name of the feast comes from its most characteristic sign, the improvised booths built in the orchards and vineyards for protection from the sun during the time of harvest. Later this agricultural festival became a memorial of Israel's exodus journey, and the booths became reminders of the nomadic shelters in which the Israelites lived during their forty years in the wilderness. The central place for its celebration was in Jerusalem at the temple. Pilgrims would come from throughout the land and from every Jewish community in the world. They came in colorful caravans—traveling by chariot, donkey, camel, and on foot—up to Jerusalem.

The scene opens on a note of profound uncertainty. The last scene had ended with many of Jesus' followers leaving him because his message was too difficult. Now we see that many of the religious leaders in Jerusalem were looking for a way to put him to death (verse 1). For that reason, Jesus decides not to join the caravan with his extended family going to Jerusalem. The "brothers" of Jesus, possibly sons of Joseph by a prior marriage or close cousins of Jesus, urge him to go for the festival in order to show himself to the world through his deeds (verses 3–4). Their advice that he go public in order "to be widely known" sounds like the satanic temptations to use his power for display, as found in the other gospels. While his brothers acknowledged that Jesus could work wonders, they did not "believe in him" (verse 5). Genuine faith requires more than seeing signs, and physical proximity to Jesus does not guarantee belief.

As a marked man, Jesus must plan his steps carefully. Though Jesus will ultimately be revealed as the Messiah, he chooses a gradual approach. He will not be pressured to act before his "time" (verses 6, 8), so Jesus went up to the feast in Jerusalem "in secret" (verse 10). The Father is the master of Jesus' destiny, and his brothers are not part of God's design. As Jesus, his disciples, "the Jews," and "the crowds" are gathered in Jerusalem, lots of questions are raised: who is Jesus, where is Jesus (verse 11), and what is he doing (verse 12)? "The Jews" are generally the religious leaders: the Pharisees, Sadducees, Sanhedrin, and that group of influential Jews who have already decided negatively against Jesus. They certainly do not represent all Jews, because the disciples and the crowds in Jerusalem are all Jewish people. Among the crowds, some were saying "he is a good man," a rather mediocre but positive response; others were saying "no, he is deceiving the crowd," a skeptical response but far short of hostile (verse 12). But none of these Jewish people would speak openly about Jesus, because they feared their religious leaders (verse 13).

In the midst of this heated conflict, Jesus begins teaching in the temple (verse 14). The issues at stake are the origins of his authority and the source of his teaching. The religious leaders question how Jesus could speak with such learning since he had no formal rabbinic training. Jesus responds, "My teaching is not mine but his who sent me" (verse 16). Like a trained rabbi, Jesus refers to the law given by Moses, in order to vindicate his own previous action of healing on the Sabbath the man who had been ill for 38 years (5:16–18). He cited two conflicting laws: the law of the Sabbath and the law of circumcision, which states that a male child should be circumcised on the eighth day after his birth. The religious leaders apparently felt that the law of circumcision took precedence and that a boy should receive circumcision even on the Sabbath if it fell on a boy's eighth day of life (verse 23). Because the Jewish teachers taught that circumcision was the perfection of a man, Jesus argues from the lesser to the greater and concluded that he was in agreement with the law for healing "a man's whole body on the Sabbath."

Reflection and Discussion

• Why would Jesus have gone up to Jerusalem for the festival of Booths even though he had told his brothers he was not going to the feast?

• In what way do the disciples, the "brothers" of Jesus, "the Jews," and "the crowds" represent different responses to him? Why did Jesus receive a mixed reception by the people of his own time?

• When have I seen religious principles put ahead of love for another? What is my approach to the law and its observance?

Prayer

Jesus, sometimes I respond to you as if you were merely a good person or a wonderworker. Give me a deeper and truer faith in you. Open my heart to you so that I will understand your teaching rightly and interpret it with compassion for all.

"You will search for me, but you will not find me;
and where I am, you cannot come." John 7:34

The Messiah Who Comes from the Father

JOHN 7:25–36 *²⁵Now some of the people of Jerusalem were saying, "Is not this the man whom they are trying to kill? ²⁶And here he is, speaking openly, but they say nothing to him! Can it be that the authorities really know that this is the Messiah? ²⁷Yet we know where this man is from; but when the Messiah comes, no one will know where he is from." ²⁸Then Jesus cried out as he was teaching in the temple, "You know me, and you know where I am from. I have not come on my own. But the one who sent me is true, and you do not know him. ²⁹I know him, because I am from him, and he sent me." ³⁰Then they tried to arrest him, but no one laid hands on him, because his hour had not yet come. ³¹Yet many in the crowd believed in him and were saying, "When the Messiah comes, will he do more signs than this man has done?"*

³²The Pharisees heard the crowd muttering such things about him, and the chief priests and Pharisees sent temple police to arrest him. ³³Jesus then said, "I will be with you a little while longer, and then I am going to him who sent me. ³⁴You will search for me, but you will not find me; and where I am, you cannot come." ³⁵The Jews said to one another, "Where does this man intend to go that we will not find him? Does he intend to go to the Dispersion among the Greeks and teach the Greeks? ³⁶What does he mean by saying, 'You will search for me and you will not find me' and 'Where I am, you cannot come'?"

The issue of this discussion in the temple is the identity of Jesus: Who is this stranger whom the religious leaders are trying to kill? The people of Jerusalem speculate that this might indeed be the Messiah. Their confusion expresses the fact that the Jewish people had a diverse variety of messianic expectations at the time. The gospel writer wants the reader to understand that Jesus fulfilled all of these various expectations in his own unique way.

One aspect of the expectancy about the Messiah involved his origin. One strain of thought in Jewish literature stated that the Messiah's origin is hidden or unknown (verse 27). Because many knew that Jesus was a Galilean from Nazareth, the people of Jerusalem presumed that he could not be the Messiah (since they knew where he was from). Yet, Jesus' true origin is not a geographical place but God himself, whom Jesus referred to as "the one who sent me" (verse 28).

As the Jewish people celebrate their loyalty to the one true God at the feast of Booths, some of them are rejecting the one sent by God. About their relationship to God, Jesus said, "you do not know him." He accuses them not only of unawareness about the Messiah, but also of lack of knowledge about the God who sent him. Since the Father is known to Jesus but unknown to them, Jesus indeed fits the messianic profile that states "no one will know where he is from."

To the religious leaders and the crowds in Jerusalem, not only the origins but also the destination of Jesus remains a mystery. Jesus said, "I am going to him who sent me" (verse 33) and "where I am, you cannot come" (verse 34). The religious leaders are unable to comprehend or enter the world of Jesus and of the Father. They no more understand where he is going than where he came from (verses 35–36). The mystery of Jesus can only be understood in terms of his origins and his destiny in God.

Jesus' words about his identity continually divide his hearers. To some he is a good man, to others he is a deceiver (verse 12); to some he might be the Messiah (verse 31), others want to arrest him (verses 30, 32). Many of the people in the crowd believe in Jesus and ask, "When the Messiah comes, will he do more signs than this man has done?" Prepared to believe that he might be the Messiah because of the signs he has done, they join a growing number who believe because of Jesus' signs.

The feast of Booths, coming at the end of the agricultural year and the end of the pilgrimage festivals, anticipates the end times and the coming of the Messiah. In those days, as Israel's prophets proclaimed, all the people of the world will go up to Jerusalem to worship God on the feast of Booths (Zech 14:16). Jesus' words and actions in the temple will transcend and transform the Jewish expectations of the Messiah expressed during this feast, not replacing but perfecting the hopes of Israel.

Reflection and Discussion

• How do the words and deeds of Jesus cause conflict and division among the people gathered in Jerusalem for the feast of Booths? Why is there such a wide range of opinions about him?

• What are my own preconceived expectations about Jesus? How is the drama of Jesus' identity continually played out today?

Prayer

Jesus Messiah, your origin is from the Father, and your destiny is to return to the Father. Correct my faulty conceptions of you so that I can come to know you more deeply and recognize your presence today.

"Let anyone who is thirsty come to me, and let the one who believes in me drink." John 7:37–38

Rivers of Living Water Flow from the Believer's Heart

JOHN 7:37–52 *37On the last day of the festival, the great day, while Jesus was standing there, he cried out, "Let anyone who is thirsty come to me, 38and let the one who believes in me drink. As the scripture has said, 'Out of the believer's heart shall flow rivers of living water.'" 39Now he said this about the Spirit, which believers in him were to receive; for as yet there was no Spirit, because Jesus was not yet glorified.*

40When they heard these words, some in the crowd said, "This is really the prophet." 41Others said, "This is the Messiah." But some asked, "Surely the Messiah does not come from Galilee, does he? 42Has not the scripture said that the Messiah is descended from David and comes from Bethlehem, the village where David lived?" 43So there was a division in the crowd because of him. 44Some of them wanted to arrest him, but no one laid hands on him.

45Then the temple police went back to the chief priests and Pharisees, who asked them, "Why did you not arrest him?" 46The police answered, "Never has anyone spoken like this!" 47Then the Pharisees replied, "Surely you have not been deceived too, have you? 48Has any one of the authorities or of the Pharisees believed in him? ⁴⁹*But this crowd, which does not know the law—they are accursed."* ⁵⁰*Nicodemus, who had gone to Jesus before, and who was one of them, asked,* ⁵¹*"Our law does not judge people without first giving them a hearing to find out what they are doing, does it?"* ⁵²*They replied, "Surely you are not also from Galilee, are you? Search and you will see that no prophet is to arise from Galilee."*

In the exodus journey, God had given miraculous food and drink to his people: abundant manna in the wilderness (Exod 16:4) and gushing water from the rock (Exod 17:6). The Psalms speak of this water flowing like a river (Ps 78:16; 105:40–41). Both the feast of Passover (6:4) and the feast of Booths (7:2) commemorate events of the exodus. Recalling God's blessings during their wilderness sojourn, Nehemiah says, "You gave your good spirit to instruct them, and did not withhold your manna from their mouths, and gave them water for their thirst (Neh 9:20).

The feast of Booths occurred just before the beginning of the rainy season. On each day of the feast, priests would walk in solemn procession from the pool of Siloam to the temple and ceremonially pour out water at the altar as a prayer that the rains would come. But the water ceremony was also an anticipation of the days of the coming Messiah, who was expected to repeat and perfect the gift of water given through Moses in the desert. In the prophets, water flows from the temple, believed to be the very center of the earth, and gives life to the desert regions all around Jerusalem (Ezek 47:1–11).

On the last day of the feast Jesus proclaimed that God would give rivers of living water to those who believe in him (verse 38). In those days, the temple will no longer be the source of these life-giving waters, but Jesus himself will be the source of living waters. The gospel explains that this flowing water is the Holy Spirit whom believers would receive after Jesus is glorified on the cross (verse 39). The life and power of the Spirit is so rich in the heart of the believer that it is like a self-replenishing and overflowing stream.

Again the self-revelation of Jesus provokes divisions among the people. Some came to a deeper faith in Jesus, calling him the great prophet and the Messiah. Others became more firm in their rejection of him, wanting to arrest him. Still others raised theological and political objections about the origins of the Messiah and insisted that Jesus did not meet the expectations. Their problem is similar to people who define happiness so narrowly that they cannot receive it when it is offered to them. They cannot understand that God is breaking out of their human standards and offering them a life that is new and abundant.

When asked by the religious leaders why they have not arrested Jesus, the temple police reply, "Never has anyone spoken like this!" (verses 45–46). In the course of their duties, they would have heard many teachers in the temple courts. It is amazing that the police did not try to blame their failure to arrest Jesus on the shifting crowds, but spoke rather of his compelling teachings. While Nicodemus urges his fellow leaders to give Jesus a fair and thorough hearing, other religious leaders have already made up their minds about Jesus. While the people of Jerusalem debate the identity of Jesus and the source of his teachings, the suspense continues, and readers continue to reflect on Jesus' claims and await the time of his glorification.

Reflection and Discussion

• How do Old Testament texts express the symbolic meaning of the water ritual in the temple during the feast of Booths?

• In what sense does Jesus himself transcend and fulfill the water ritual of the feast of Booths?

• How have I experienced the abundance of the Holy Spirit flowing within me? Are my expectations too narrow to experience God's gifts fully?

• It is ironic that those who boast of their scriptural expertise are ignorant of who Jesus is, while the people in the crowds who are said to be biblically illiterate begin to believe that he is the Messiah. What does this reality say about the way we read and study Scripture?

• What is the meaning for me of Jesus' proclamation in verse 38? What is the relationship between believing in Jesus and experiencing the refreshing presence of the Holy Spirit?

Prayer

Source of Living Water, you quench my deepest thirsts. Open my heart so that the waters of life may flow through me, cleansing, refreshing, and giving me abundant life in your Holy Spirit.

"Let anyone among you who is without sin
be the first to throw a stone at her." John 8:7

The Woman Judged
Forgiven by Jesus

JOHN 8:1–11 ¹*Then each of them went home, while Jesus went to the Mount of Olives.* ²*Early in the morning he came again to the temple. All the people came to him and he sat down and began to teach them.* ³*The scribes and the Pharisees brought a woman who had been caught in adultery; and making her stand before all of them,* ⁴*they said to him, "Teacher, this woman was caught in the very act of committing adultery.* ⁵*Now in the law Moses commanded us to stone such women. Now what do you say?"* ⁶*They said this to test him, so that they might have some charge to bring against him. Jesus bent down and wrote with his finger on the ground.* ⁷*When they kept on questioning him, he straightened up and said to them, "Let anyone among you who is without sin be the first to throw a stone at her."* ⁸*And once again he bent down and wrote on the ground.* ⁹*When they heard it, they went away, one by one, beginning with the elders; and Jesus was left alone with the woman standing before him.* ¹⁰*Jesus straightened up and said to her, "Woman, where are they? Has no one condemned you?"* ¹¹*She said, "No one, sir." And Jesus said, "Neither do I condemn you. Go your way, and from now on do not sin again."*

This account of Jesus and the woman is an addition, and not an original part of the gospel. Because of its unique vocabulary, the way it interrupts the narrative flow of the Feast of Booths, and its absence from the oldest manuscripts of the gospel, scholars are convinced that it was not written by the evangelist but was later added to the gospel. This free-floating passage, however, was treasured by the church in the early centuries and eventually ended here in John's gospel. For this reason, many editions of the Bible set off this passage in brackets within the gospel text.

The usual commentary on this scene focuses on the woman and issues of sexual sin. But the text demonstrates that those who are motivated by judgmental attitudes, wishing to condemn the woman, are equally the focus of the narrative. The woman's accusers state that she has been "caught in the very act of committing adultery" (verse 4). The religious leaders clearly have no real concern for the fate of the woman. They were out to get Jesus. Neither do they care about the injured husband or the partner in adultery, who has apparently gotten off scot free. The law of Moses, to which the accusers refer, prescribes the death penalty for both the man and the woman involved (Lev 20:10; Deut 22:22–24). Clearly, concern for the woman is not the issue for these men. The woman seems to be merely a prop in the scene, exhibit A at the trial.

The gospel writer unfolds this story in two parallel scenes, each beginning when Jesus bends down and writes on the ground (verses 6, 8). This gesture can be understood as a sign of the tranquil confidence of Jesus, who refused to enter the zealous fervor of the woman's accusers. Each time he rises from the ground, he pronounces a pivotal verse of the narrative. He speaks first to the scribes and Pharisees about sin: "Let anyone among you who is without sin be the first to throw a stone at her" (verse 7). The accusers become the accused and gradually walk away. When Jesus rises again from the ground, he is left alone with the woman and is the first person to speak to her directly in the narrative. She is no longer an objective exhibit at a trial, but she is a person who can enter into a relationship with Jesus. The forgiveness of Jesus gives her the opportunity to live a new life. Not only has Jesus saved her physical life from those who would stone her, but also he offers her the possibility of a genuine life in a right relationship with God (verse 11).

Reflection and Discussion

• From what types of imprisonment does Jesus free both the woman and the religious officials? In what way does judgmentalism provide the fuel for racism, sexism, and neglect of the poor?

• Earlier the gospel proclaimed that God did not send his Son into the world to "condemn" but that the world might be "saved" (3:17). What is the thought of Jesus when I stand before him with my sins? What does he offer me?

• How does this scene demonstrate Jesus' delicate balance between the justice of not condoning the sin and the mercy of forgiving sinners?

Prayer

Just and merciful Lord, you forgave the sinful woman and the judgmental men. Help me to realize the depths of my sin and the liberation you offer me through your forgiveness. Continue to transform my life with your healing grace.

> "When you have lifted up the Son of Man, then you will realize
> that I am he, and that I do nothing on my own, but I speak
> these things as the Father instructed me." John 8:28

The Light of the World
Scatters the Darkness of Sin

JOHN 8:12–30 *¹²Again Jesus spoke to them, saying, "I am the light of the world. Whoever follows me will never walk in darkness but will have the light of life." ¹³Then the Pharisees said to him, "You are testifying on your own behalf; your testimony is not valid." ¹⁴Jesus answered, "Even if I testify on my own behalf, my testimony is valid because I know where I have come from and where I am going, but you do not know where I come from or where I am going. ¹⁵You judge by human standards; I judge no one. ¹⁶Yet even if I do judge, my judgment is valid; for it is not I alone who judge, but I and the Father who sent me. ¹⁷In your law it is written that the testimony of two witnesses is valid. ¹⁸I testify on my own behalf, and the Father who sent me testifies on my behalf." ¹⁹Then they said to him, "Where is your Father?" Jesus answered, "You know neither me nor my Father. If you knew me, you would know my Father also." ²⁰He spoke these words while he was teaching in the treasury of the temple, but no one arrested him, because his hour had not yet come.*

²¹Again he said to them, "I am going away, and you will search for me, but you will die in your sin. Where I am going, you cannot come." ²²Then the Jews said, "Is he going to kill himself? Is that what he means by saying, 'Where I am going, you cannot come'?" [23]*He said to them, "You are from below, I am from above; you are of this world, I am not of this world.* [24]*I told you that you would die in your sins, for you will die in your sins unless you believe that I am he."* [25]*They said to him, "Who are you?" Jesus said to them, "Why do I speak to you at all?* [26]*I have much to say about you and much to condemn; but the one who sent me is true, and I declare to the world what I have heard from him."* [27]*They did not understand that he was speaking to them about the Father.* [28]*So Jesus said, "When you have lifted up the Son of Man, then you will realize that I am he, and that I do nothing on my own, but I speak these things as the Father instructed me.* [29]*And the one who sent me is with me; he has not left me alone, for I always do what is pleasing to him."* [30]*As he was saying these things, many believed in him.*

During each evening of the feast of Booths, torches were lit, making the temple the light of Jerusalem. In this context, Jesus resumed his discourse and proclaimed, "I am the light of the world." Those who follow him will not walk in darkness, but will have the "light of life" (verse 12). As the feast of Booths commemorated Israel's wandering in the desert, the light recalled the pillar of fire that manifested God's presence and led his people to freedom. Not only is Jesus the bread (John 6) and the living water (John 7), he is also the light. Here John continues the exodus theme and presents Jesus as the completion of God's saving deeds for his people. Jewish literature had declared that the law given to Moses was the light given to the world (Wis 18:4). What the Torah once was for Israel, Jesus is now to the world. He will lead his followers from the darkness into the fullness of freedom and life. Jesus is the perfection of the Torah's light and the personification of the temple's light.

The presence of Jesus calls for a decision: either to remain in the darkness or to walk in the light of life by following him. The acceptance or refusal of his testimony depends on whether one knows where Jesus has come from and where he is going (verse 14). The religious leaders attack Jesus' witness to the Father because they "judge by human standards," accepting only what they can see, touch, and control (verse 15). They remain in the darkness of spiritual blindness, refusing to see the light of his true identity and set on bringing charges against him. Jesus has come from the Father, and his words and actions conform to the mission given to him by the Father. But the Jewish leaders are not open to his words on either his origins or his destiny with the Father, a reality beyond their darkened sight and impaired judgment. Because of their closed-mindedness, they are ignorant of who Jesus is and who his Father is, for to know one is to know the other (verse 19).

During the Israelites' exodus, they would have died in the wilderness if they had not been led by the God revealed to them as "I Am." Here Jesus proclaims that he is that saving divine presence for God's people: "You will die in your sins unless you believe that I am he" (verse 24). This note of hope assures his listeners that the division between what is "from below" and what is "from above" need not be absolute (verse 23). Jesus has come from the Father in order that people may be lifted up to him. If they believe that Jesus is the revelation of the Father, they will bridge the gulf between what is "from below" and "from above."

The fullness of Jesus' saving presence will be revealed when he is lifted up on the cross: "When you have lifted up the Son of Man, then you will realize that I am he" (verse 28). Jesus defines himself as the one in whom the God of exodus is present to save once again. In the elevation of Jesus on the cross, the revelation of God will take place, and the listeners will know the oneness of the Father and the Son. Jesus has been sent by the Father and will return to the Father by way of the cross. Those who will die in their disbelief cannot come where Jesus is going (verse 21), but those who believe that he is the way to true life will follow Jesus on the way that leads to eternal life. As Jesus spoke these words, many in his audience believed in him (verse 30).

Reflection and Discussion

• What feelings do I associate with darkness? What parts of my life are still in darkness?

• What is the meaning of Jesus' testimony: "I am the Light of the world"? In what way does the presence of Jesus call for a personal decision?

• In what sense do I judge "from below," by human standards? What could elevate my faith in Jesus?

• What does Jesus claim about his relationship with the Father? How does knowing Jesus lead people to eternal life?

Prayer

Light of the World, you lead your people out of darkness into the light of life. Shine in the dark corners of my life, and light my way to the Father. Help me to be a light-bearer for others along the way.

"If you continue in my word, you are truly my disciples; and you will know the truth, and the truth will make you free." John 8:31–32

The One Who Was Before Abraham

JOHN 8:31–59 [31]*Then Jesus said to the Jews who had believed in him, "If you continue in my word, you are truly my disciples;* [32]*and you will know the truth, and the truth will make you free."* [33]*They answered him, "We are descendants of Abraham and have never been slaves to anyone. What do you mean by saying, 'You will be made free'?"*

[34]*Jesus answered them, "Very truly, I tell you, everyone who commits sin is a slave to sin.* [35]*The slave does not have a permanent place in the household; the son has a place there forever.* [36]*So if the Son makes you free, you will be free indeed.* [37]*I know that you are descendants of Abraham; yet you look for an opportunity to kill me, because there is no place in you for my word.* [38]*I declare what I have seen in the Father's presence; as for you, you should do what you have heard from the Father."*

[39]*They answered him, "Abraham is our father." Jesus said to them, "If you were Abraham's children, you would be doing what Abraham did,* [40]*but now you are trying to kill me, a man who has told you the truth that I heard from God. This is not what Abraham did.* [41]*You are indeed doing what your father does." They said to him, "We are not illegitimate children; we have one father, God himself."* [42]*Jesus said to them, "If God were your Father, you would love me, for I came*

96

*from God and now I am here. I did not come on my own, but he sent me. *[43]*Why do you not understand what I say? It is because you cannot accept my word. *[44]*You are from your father the devil, and you choose to do your father's desires. He was a murderer from the beginning and does not stand in the truth, because there is no truth in him. When he lies, he speaks according to his own nature, for he is a liar and the father of lies. *[45]*But because I tell the truth, you do not believe me. *[46]*Which of you convicts me of sin? If I tell the truth, why do you not believe me? *[47]*Whoever is from God hears the words of God. The reason you do not hear them is that you are not from God."*

[48]*The Jews answered him, "Are we not right in saying that you are a Samaritan and have a demon?" *[49]*Jesus answered, "I do not have a demon; but I honor my Father, and you dishonor me. *[50]*Yet I do not seek my own glory; there is one who seeks it and he is the judge. *[51]*Very truly, I tell you, whoever keeps my word will never see death." *[52]*The Jews said to him, "Now we know that you have a demon. Abraham died, and so did the prophets; yet you say, 'Whoever keeps my word will never taste death.' *[53]*Are you greater than our father Abraham, who died? The prophets also died. Who do you claim to be?" *[54]*Jesus answered, "If I glorify myself, my glory is nothing. It is my Father who glorifies me, he of whom you say, 'He is our God,' *[55]*though you do not know him. But I know him; if I would say that I do not know him, I would be a liar like you. But I do know him and I keep his word. *[56]*Your ancestor Abraham rejoiced that he would see my day; he saw it and was glad." *[57]*Then the Jews said to him, "You are not yet fifty years old, and have you seen Abraham?" *[58]*Jesus said to them, "Very truly, I tell you, before Abraham was, I am." *[59]*So they picked up stones to throw at him, but Jesus hid himself and went out of the temple.*

Jesus addresses these words to the Jews who had begun to believe in him. Jesus recognizes the tentative nature of their faith and invites them to true discipleship. Jesus says, "If you continue in my word, you are truly my disciples" (verse 31). The word translated "continue" also means "remain" or "abide." The word of Jesus, his revelation of the Father, is not a message that can be embraced quickly or easily. Jesus is asking them to live with his word so that gradually the vision and direction of their lives will change. They will truly be disciples as they abide in Jesus' word, creating a space for that word and living with it so that it transforms their lives.

When they abide with Jesus' word, they will come to know the truth, and the truth will make them free (verse 32). This "truth" is far more than an intellectual knowledge. It is a rich and ancient concept of knowing that engages the whole person in a profound acceptance. The freedom that results from such a personal welcome of Jesus' word is a deep confidence and interior freedom that results from an intimate relationship with God.

The Jewish believers resist Jesus' invitation to discipleship. They state that they are already free as descendants of Abraham (verse 39). Jesus responds that while they may be physical descendants of Abraham, they are neither spiritually nor ethically children of Abraham. Unlike Abraham they have not opened their lives to the transforming power of God's word. Their actions indicate that they are not children of God, but allied with the forces opposed to God and truth (verses 44–47).

The language used in this encounter is strong and personal. When Jesus accuses some of the crowd of being children of the devil, it is not because they are Jews. After all, Jesus himself and his disciples were Jews. Rather he is challenging those of any race and time who close their eyes to the life-giving truth that he offers. The language is strong because the stakes are so high. The word of Jesus brings light and life; those who reject it choose darkness and death.

Having proclaimed that abiding in his word brings knowledge of the truth and genuine freedom (verses 31–32), Jesus proclaims another astonishing promise: "Very truly, I tell you, whoever keeps my word will never see death" (verse 51). Remaining in the word of Jesus, living out its demands, taking it to heart, leads to the quality of life that lasts forever.

Again the words of Jesus are rejected by an appeal to Abraham (verses 52–53). Jesus responds by announcing that Abraham looked forward to this day (verse 56), the day when all peoples would be blessed through Abraham's offspring (Gen 12:3). Jesus justifies his promise with another amazing claim: "Very truly, I tell you, before Abraham was, I am" (verse 58). Having read the first chapter of the gospel, we know that Jesus is indeed the eternal Word, existing with God from eternity. He speaks with the voice of the God of Abraham, Isaac, and Jacob, the God of the living. Jesus is the source of life and hope even for Abraham and the prophets. This claim to divinity was too much for the crowd, who rejected his message and took up stones to cast at this blasphemer.

Reflection and Discussion

• What are some false understandings of freedom today? What is the relationship between truth and freedom?

• What is the meaning of Jesus' statement: "The truth will make you free"? How has his word brought me freedom?

• How does Jesus fulfill the hopes of Abraham? How does Jesus fulfill the deepest hopes of all people? Do I trust my future to him?

Prayer

Lord Jesus, open my ears to hear your word, and open my heart to accept it. Remove from my life all that would distort your word so that I can experience the true freedom that comes from living in your truth. Make me secure in your promises, and lead me to eternal life.

SUGGESTIONS FOR FACILITATORS, GROUP SESSION 5

1. Welcome group members and ask if anyone has any questions, announcements, or requests.

2. You may want to pray this prayer as a group:

Father in heaven, help us to know Jesus through the gospel so that we will understand that his origin is from you and that his destiny is to return to you. As the Bread of Life, may he nourish us with his presence along our life's journey. As the Source of Living Water, may he quench our deepest thirsts and send your Spirit to cleanse and refresh us. As the Light of the World, may he shine in the dark corners of our lives and light our way to you. Open our minds and hearts so that we will understand his teaching rightly and accept it completely. May his truth set us free.

3. Ask one or more of the following questions:
   - What most intrigued you from this week's study?
   - What makes you want to know and understand more of God's word?

4. Discuss lessons 19 through 24. Choose one or more of the questions for reflection and discussion from each lesson to talk over as a group.

5. Ask the group members to name one thing they have most appreciated about the way the group has worked during this Bible study. Ask group members to discuss any changes they might suggest in the way the group works in future studies.

6. Invite group members to complete lessons 25 through 30 on their own during the six days before the next meeting. They should write out their own answers to the questions as preparation for next week's session.

7. Ask group members why they think that John's gospel teaches about Jesus through the use of his "I am" titles. Discuss which of these many identifying titles challenges them the most.

8. Conclude by praying aloud together the prayer at the end of one of the lessons discussed. You may want to conclude the prayer by asking members to voice prayers of thanksgiving.

"Neither this man nor his parents sinned; he was born blind that God's work might be revealed in him." John 9:3

The Light of the World Gives Sight to the Blind

JOHN 9:1–12 ¹*As he walked along, he saw a man blind from birth.* ²*His disciples asked him, "Rabbi, who sinned, this man or his parents, that he was born blind?"* ³*Jesus answered, "Neither this man nor his parents sinned; he was born blind so that God's works might be revealed in him.* ⁴*We must work the works of him who sent me while it is day; night is coming when no one can work.* ⁵*As long as I am in the world, I am the light of the world."* ⁶*When he had said this, he spat on the ground and made mud with the saliva and spread the mud on the man's eyes,* ⁷*saying to him, "Go, wash in the pool of Siloam" (which means Sent). Then he went and washed and came back able to see.* ⁸*The neighbors and those who had seen him before as a beggar began to ask, "Is this not the man who used to sit and beg?"* ⁹*Some were saying, "It is he." Others were saying, "No, but it is someone like him." He kept saying, "I am the man."* ¹⁰*But they kept asking him, "Then how were your eyes opened?"* ¹¹*He answered, "The man called Jesus made mud, spread it on my eyes, and said to me, 'Go to Siloam and wash.' Then I went and washed and received my sight."* ¹²*They said to him, "Where is he?" He said, "I do not know."*

The narrative focuses on the fact that this man had been "blind from birth." Assuming that congenital blindness was some kind of punishment for sin, the disciples inquire into its cause. Jesus, rejecting the alternatives posed by the question, shifts the focus from the cause of his affliction to its purpose—"so that God's works might be revealed in him" (verse 3).

The healing itself is told with vivid and factual details (verses 6–7). Jesus spits on the ground to make a ball of mud that he smears on the man's eyes. Then he sends him to the pool of Siloam to wash the mud away. Such procedures were not uncommon among ancient healers. The man's obedient response to the word of Jesus is indicated by simple verbs: he went, he washed, and he came back able to see.

In addition to its accurate details, the writer molds the description into a profoundly symbolic narrative. By working this sign, Jesus will show himself to be "the light of the world" (verse 5). The account contrasts the blind man's gaining of sight with the spiritual blindness of the religious leaders. The context of the feast of Booths is still apparent, and the waters of Siloam are vital for its rituals. Yet, the writer notes that Siloam means "Sent," indicating that the One Sent by God is the true cause of the blind man's cure. As the living water and the light of the world, Jesus gives both sight and insight to the man who was blind.

If the man is blind from birth, then the restoring of his sight is nothing less than a new birth. He is indeed born again from above (3:3), as he comes from the darkness into the light. Bishop Irenaeus, writing in the second century, proposed that "God's work" (verse 3) manifested in this miracle of Jesus is "the fashioning of man" as at the Creation, by which "the Lord took clay from the earth and formed man." What the Word "had omitted to form in the womb"— that is, the man's eyes—he "supplied in public, that the works of God might be manifested in him." The washing in the waters of Siloam is the "laver of regeneration," the new birth of Christian baptism. The man born blind is truly reborn of water and Spirit (3:5).

The healing of the blind man is the sixth of Jesus' seven signs in John's gospel. It continues the gospel's agenda of showing Jesus to be the Word Made Flesh and God's Messiah. The parallels with the healing of the lame man (John 5) are evident. The sites for both healings are pools, both are worked on the Sabbath, and both are extraordinary due to the length of time the men had suffered from the malady. Yet, as the narrative unfolds, we will see that the responses of each man could not be more different.

Reflection and Discussion

• How does Jesus respond to the suggestion that we are somehow responsible for our afflictions, that God punishes us with suffering?

• What part of my life is yet unformed and in need of fashioning? How can I let Jesus heal me and make me whole?

• What indicates that the gospel writer has formed this account into a sign of Jesus' identity and mission, rather than as simply a miraculous event.

Prayer

Light of the World, touch my eyes that I may see clearly, and enlighten my soul so that I may believe in you. Continue to re-create me so that God's work may be manifested in my life.

"He put mud on my eyes. Then I washed, and now I see."

John 9:15

Interrogation of the Man Healed on the Sabbath

JOHN 9:13–23 ¹³*They brought to the Pharisees the man who had formerly been blind.* ¹⁴*Now it was a sabbath day when Jesus made the mud and opened his eyes.* ¹⁵*Then the Pharisees also began to ask him how he had received his sight. He said to them, "He put mud on my eyes. Then I washed, and now I see."* ¹⁶*Some of the Pharisees said, "This man is not from God, for he does not observe the sabbath." But others said, "How can a man who is a sinner perform such signs?" And they were divided.* ¹⁷*So they said again to the blind man, "What do you say about him? It was your eyes he opened." He said, "He is a prophet."*

¹⁸*The Jews did not believe that he had been blind and had received his sight until they called the parents of the man who had received his sight* ¹⁹*and asked them, "Is this your son, who you say was born blind? How then does he now see?"* ²⁰*His parents answered, "We know that this is our son, and that he was born blind;* ²¹*but we do not know how it is that now he sees, nor do we know who opened his eyes. Ask him; he is of age. He will speak for himself."* ²²*His parents said this because they were afraid of the Jews; for the Jews had already agreed that anyone who confessed Jesus to be the Messiah would be put out of the synagogue.* ²³*Therefore his parents said, "He is of age; ask him."*

When the man healed of his blindness is brought to the religious leaders, the spotlight turns to Jesus and an investigation begins. Asked to recount how he had received his sight, the man stated the facts: "He put mud on my eyes. Then I washed, and now I see." The Pharisees were clearly divided about Jesus. Some were saying, "This man is not from God, for he does not observe the Sabbath." Surely he could have waited until the next day to heal the man. Jesus had kneaded the clay with his saliva to make mud, and kneading was among the types of work forbidden on the Sabbath. Others among the Pharisees were saying, "How can a man who is a sinner perform such signs?" Surely one opposed to God could not do such a good and wonderful deed.

When the man himself is asked his assessment of the man who healed him, the man arrived at a verdict similar to that of the Samaritan woman: "He is a prophet" (verse 17; 4:19). In a further effort to review the facts of the case to find some inconsistency, the Pharisees send for his parents. They confirm that he was born blind, but they deny knowing how it is that he now sees (verse 21). Despite their plea of ignorance, the parents seem to know more than they choose to divulge. They do not want to be dragged into the debate because of their fear of the religious authorities, for the Pharisees had already declared that anyone confessing Jesus as the Messiah would be expelled from the synagogue (verse 22). Eviction from the synagogue, the center of Jewish religious and social life, meant severe social exclusion.

Why does Jesus seem to perform so many of his miracles on the Sabbath? Surely he could have easily chosen some other day and avoided a lot of controversy from his detractors. The gospel has just recounted this wondrous healing of the man who was blind from birth, but then the writer adds, "now it was the Sabbath day when Jesus made the mud and opened his eyes" (verse 14). We know immediately that the wonder and gratitude that fill the scene will be sidetracked and extinguished by this seemingly absurd discussion of healing on the Sabbath.

But don't we do the same thing? In our parishes we overlook the powerful grace of the sacraments we share, and focus on the divisive issues that seem so trivial in comparison. In our families we take for granted the joy of sharing life with those we love, and we get hung up on the petty issues that lead to arguments. We do it with ourselves too, by ignoring our gifts and talents, while we obsess over our minor faults.

The gospel writer wants us to take note of the ridiculousness of this discussion because he wanted the church of his day to transcend this kind of divisiveness. The fact that we haven't changed much in two thousand years is probably all too obvious. But the gospel presents us with a higher calling: the inspiration and grace to overcome our sinful and petty nature, and the glorious task of transforming our lives in Christ. The word of Jesus calls us to transcend our fears and small-mindedness and live in the freedom of the truth.

Reflection and Discussion

• If Jesus honored the Sabbath as a faithful Jew, why would he choose to heal on the Sabbath?

• In what ways do I ignore the big picture of God's grace and obsess about minute trivialities? What does this narrative challenge me to change about myself, my family, or my church?

Prayer

Lord Jesus, you want to give me a vision of how wide and wonderful life can be, yet I insist on wearing blinders. Open my eyes to the wonders you offer me so that I will know the truth that can set me free.

"Surely we are not blind, are we?"
John 9:40

The Blindness
of Those Who See

JOHN 9:24–41 ²⁴So for the second time they called the man who had been blind, and they said to him, "Give glory to God! We know that this man is a sinner." ²⁵He answered, "I do not know whether he is a sinner. One thing I do know, that though I was blind, now I see." ²⁶They said to him, "What did he do to you? How did he open your eyes?" ²⁷He answered them, "I have told you already, and you would not listen. Why do you want to hear it again? Do you also want to become his disciples?" ²⁸Then they reviled him, saying, "You are his disciple, but we are disciples of Moses. ²⁹We know that God has spoken to Moses, but as for this man, we do not know where he comes from." ³⁰The man answered, "Here is an astonishing thing! You do not know where he comes from, and yet he opened my eyes. ³¹We know that God does not listen to sinners, but he does listen to one who worships him and obeys his will. ³²Never since the world began has it been heard that anyone opened the eyes of a person born blind. ³³If this man were not from God, he could do nothing." ³⁴They answered him, "You were born entirely in sins, and are you trying to teach us?" And they drove him out.

³⁵Jesus heard that they had driven him out, and when he found him, he said, "Do you believe in the Son of Man?" ³⁶He answered, "And who is he, sir? Tell me, so that I may believe in him." ³⁷Jesus said to him, "You have seen him, and the

*one speaking with you is he." *[38]*He said, "Lord, I believe." And he worshiped him.* [39]*Jesus said, "I came into this world for judgment so that those who do not see may see, and those who do see may become blind." *[40]*Some of the Pharisees near him heard this and said to him, "Surely we are not blind, are we?" *[41]*Jesus said to them, "If you were blind, you would not have sin. But now that you say, 'We see,' your sin remains.*

The man born blind points out the absurdity of the opponents' position with his quick and ready wit. While the religious leaders convince themselves that Jesus is a sinner, the man points to the clear evidence, "One thing I do know, that though I was blind, now I see" (verse 25). When he is asked to recount his healing again, the man balks, "Why do you want to hear it again?" Then with a quick ironic reply, he challenged them, "Do you also want to become his disciples?" (verse 27). When the opponents question the origins of Jesus, the man responds with a sarcastic wit, "Here is an astonishing thing! You do not know where he comes from, and yet he opened my eyes" (verse 30). The healed man has seen through the attempts of the Pharisees to trip him up. His illogical debate with the Pharisees clarifies his faith in Jesus as it becomes ever more clear to him that Jesus is truly from God.

The Pharisees, on the other hand, have secured their place in the former gift of God that came through Moses, and they reject the perfection of that gift that comes through Jesus the Messiah. They insist that Jesus is a sinner (verse 24) and that the man's blindness from birth indicates that he was "born entirely in sins" (verse 34). The healed man insists that someone who opened the eyes of a man born blind must be from God: "We know that God does not listen to sinners, but he does listen to one who worships him and obeys his will" (verse 31). Insisting that God must be the source of his own new birth, the healed man shows that the religious leaders are incapable of seeing and assessing the work of God among them. Because the Pharisees cannot bear the truth that he represents, they expel him from the synagogue.

After the healed man's debate with his opponents, Jesus himself finds the man and finally encounters him in person (verse 35). As far as we know, the man born blind had never laid eyes on Jesus (remember he had to first go wash in the pool before he could see). When Jesus reveals himself as the one who had opened the man's eyes, the former blind man believes and falls at Jesus' feet in worship (verse 38). The man not only received physical sight, but has also progressively grown in spiritual insight. Beginning by speaking of a "man called Jesus" (verse 11), he then hailed Jesus as "a prophet" (verse 17), and then became convinced that Jesus came from God (verse 33). When Jesus asked him if he believed in the Son of Man (verse 35), the man responded, "Lord, I believe" (verse 38). By believing and worshiping Jesus, the man truly "sees," in the fullest sense of the term.

This sixth sign in the gospel becomes a message about sight and blindness in the spiritual realm. Jesus has come into the world so that those who believe may come to see and to recognize the blindness of those who refuse to believe. As the incarnation of the Word of God, Jesus makes God known when he speaks and acts. The query of the Pharisees, "Surely we are not blind, are we?" is a question to be pondered by all readers of the gospel. The truest blindness is the refusal to believe by those who are wise in their own eyes.

Reflection and Discussion

• What is the fuller meaning of this sign concerning blindness and sight? What is the writer teaching the reader?

• How is my vision? What are my blind spots? What could I do to correct my vision?

• How has the man's insight into the identity of Jesus changed and deepened in this account?

• How has my insight into the identity of Jesus changed and deepened through the years?

• In what sense are the Pharisees blind? Why are they unable to "see" the Light of the World?

Prayer

Light of the World, thank you for healing my vision so that I can see the way to follow you. Give me the courage to worship you and to witness your presence so that others may come to believe in you.

"The thief comes only to steal and kill and destroy.
I came that they may have life, and have it abundantly."
John 10:10

The Shepherd Gives Life to His Flock

JOHN 10:1–10 ¹*"Very truly, I tell you, anyone who does not enter the sheepfold by the gate but climbs in by another way is a thief and a bandit. ²The one who enters by the gate is the shepherd of the sheep. ³The gatekeeper opens the gate for him, and the sheep hear his voice. He calls his own sheep by name and leads them out. ⁴When he has brought out all his own, he goes ahead of them, and the sheep follow him because they know his voice. ⁵They will not follow a stranger, but they will run from him because they do not know the voice of strangers." ⁶Jesus used this figure of speech with them, but they did not understand what he was saying to them.*

⁷*So again Jesus said to them, "Very truly, I tell you, I am the gate for the sheep. ⁸All who came before me are thieves and bandits; but the sheep did not listen to them. ⁹I am the gate. Whoever enters by me will be saved, and will come in and go out and find pasture. ¹⁰The thief comes only to steal and kill and destroy. I came that they may have life, and have it abundantly.*

This is the closest Jesus will come in John's gospel to telling a parable. Actually Jesus draws on the imagery of shepherding in the ancient world to provide the backdrop for an extended reflection. During the rainy season the sheep remained in one locale where the grass was plentiful, and at night they would be led into a corral where they would be kept safe from wild animals. There were two ways to enter a sheepfold, depending on whether one wished to shepherd the sheep or do harm to them. The one who enters by deception is a thief; the one who enters through the gate is the shepherd (verses 1–2). The gatekeeper has no hesitation in letting the true shepherd into the fold (verse 3). Each sheep responds to the familiar voice of the shepherd, who calls each sheep by its own familiar name. The shepherd walks ahead of the sheep to bring them to pasture, each following the one whose voice is familiar to them (verse 4). In the case of a stranger, whose voice the sheep do not know, the sheep will not follow, but they will flee in panic (verse 5).

This imagery of shepherding provides the backdrop from which the rest of the discourse is formed. Jesus takes these images and uses them to form metaphors which establish two more "I am" sayings. The care and intimacy of these images provide beautiful illustrations of the bond of trust and familiarity that exists between Jesus and his followers. Such imagery is common in the Old Testament as an expression of how God provides for his people. Psalm 23 expresses God's care from the point of view of the flock. The psalmist proclaims that God offers everything the sheep needs for an abundant life.

Jesus first proclaims, "I am the gate for the sheep" (verse 7). He presents himself as the gateway for his flock. The opposing religious leaders are thieves and bandits, as was demonstrated by their treatment of the man born blind. In contrast to these, Jesus is the way through which the sheep are protected and the way of access to good pasture (verse 9). He is the mediator who will provide them with what they need and desire: both secure protection and abundant nourishment. He came for the sake of his followers, "that they may have life, and have it abundantly" (verse 10). This full and abundant life is salvation, the eternal life which begins already in the here and now.

Reflection and Discussion

• In what ways do these images of shepherding illustrate the experience of the man born blind and those who opposed him?

• Who or what are the strangers, thieves, and bandits who threaten me with harm? How do I experience the protection of Jesus?

• Why do I choose to follow Jesus rather than another? What is the meaning of Jesus' promise in verse 10?

Prayer

Gateway for the Sheep, you offer me security and protect me from danger. You are the way to the green pastures of abundant life. Guard me from the deceptions of those who offer me another way to live.

"I am the good shepherd. I know my own and my own know me,
just as the Father knows me and I know the Father." John 10:14–15

The Good Shepherd Lays Down His Life for the Sheep

JOHN 10:11–21 ¹¹*"I am the good shepherd. The good shepherd lays down his life for the sheep.* ¹²*The hired hand, who is not the shepherd and does not own the sheep, sees the wolf coming and leaves the sheep and runs away—and the wolf snatches them and scatters them.* ¹³*The hired hand runs away because a hired hand does not care for the sheep.* ¹⁴*I am the good shepherd. I know my own and my own know me,* ¹⁵*just as the Father knows me and I know the Father. And I lay down my life for the sheep.* ¹⁶*I have other sheep that do not belong to this fold. I must bring them also, and they will listen to my voice. So there will be one flock, one shepherd.* ¹⁷*For this reason the Father loves me, because I lay down my life in order to take it up again.* ¹⁸*No one takes it from me, but I lay it down of my own accord. I have power to lay it down, and I have power to take it up again. I have received this command from my Father."*

¹⁹*Again the Jews were divided because of these words.* ²⁰*Many of them were saying, "He has a demon and is out of his mind. Why listen to him?"* ²¹*Others were saying, "These are not the words of one who has a demon. Can a demon open the eyes of the blind?"*

The contrast between Jesus and his religious opponents continues as Jesus proclaims, "I am the good shepherd." There is a strong tradition in the Old Testament of presenting unfaithful leaders of Israel as bad shepherds who scatter their flock and consign them to the wolves (Jer 23:1–4; Ezek 34:1–10). In contrast, God is repeatedly spoken of as the true shepherd of his people. Following the exile, Ezekiel spoke of God as the good shepherd of the future who would seek out the lost, rescue and heal them, and gather them together (Ezek 34:11–16). As the monarchy of Israel disappeared, the prophets spoke of a future messianic figure who would shepherd God's people like King David (Ezek 34:23–24; 37:24).

Jesus is the true shepherd, the one who knows, gathers, and protects the sheep. The most outstanding characteristic of this good shepherd, a unique characteristic that transcends even the images from the prophets, is that he "lays down his life for his sheep" (verses 11, 15). This total dedication and self-sacrificing of the good shepherd clearly distinguishes him from the hireling who is motivated by personal gain and will abandon the flock in times of danger (verses 12–13).

Through the shepherd's ultimate sacrifice for his sheep, the world outside Israel will be drawn into the fold so that there will be "one flock, one shepherd" (verse 16). The "other sheep that do not belong to this fold" are Gentiles, those outside the sheepfold of historic Israel. Jesus clearly envisions a mission to the Gentiles following his self-sacrifice on the cross. Though it will be carried out by his disciples, it will clearly be the work of Jesus from his exalted position with the Father. Jesus' "own" sheep and his "other" sheep describe the full extent of the Christian mission, both present and future. The one flock with one shepherd refers to the one messianic community, the whole church.

In the sacrifice of the good shepherd, the Father's love for him is truly present and revealed to the world. Jesus lays down his life "in order to take it up again" (verse 17). The love of the shepherd, manifested in his power to "lay it down" and "take it up again" (verse 18), is the story that lies ahead in the second half of the gospel. The mystery of his origins and his destiny will be revealed in the suffering, death, and resurrection of Jesus.

The narrative of the feast of Booths has presented Jesus as the living water for those who thirst, the light of the world, and the good shepherd who lays down his life to gather his sheep into one fold. During the period in which

John's gospel was written, Rabbinic Judaism produced 2 Baruch to address the crisis of the destruction of Jerusalem and its temple in AD 70. It insisted that holding fast to the law given through Moses would provide an abiding presence of shepherds, light, and water: "Shepherds and lamps and fountains came from the Law and when we go away, the Law will abide. If you, therefore, look upon the Law and are intent upon wisdom, then the lamp will not be wanting and the shepherd will not give way and the fountain will not dry up" (2 Bar 77:15–16). The Christians of John's community know that God has perfected these gifts through Jesus the Messiah. The ancient symbols of Israel's temple and feasts have become flesh in Jesus, and all who believe in him share in the blessings of God.

Reflection and Discussion

• In what way do the prophets of the Old Testament help me understand the image of Jesus as the good shepherd?

• What does the image of one flock with one shepherd teach me about God's desire for the church?

• What is the most striking characteristic of the good shepherd, which transcends even the images from the prophets (verses 11, 15)? How does this characteristic convince me that Jesus is the true Shepherd?

•Who were the "other sheep" in the days of Jesus (verse 16)? Who could be the "other sheep" today?

• What is the most reassuring part of this passage for me? What do I want to remember and contemplate?

Prayer

Good Shepherd, you rescue, heal, protect, and gather your flock. Thank you for your sacrificial care for me and for the ultimate gift of laying down your life to save me from death.

"Even though you do not believe me, believe the works,
so that you may know and understand that the Father
is in me and I am in the Father." John 10:38

The Choice to Believe in Jesus

JOHN 10: 22–42 ²²*At that time the festival of the Dedication took place in Jerusalem. It was winter,* ²³*and Jesus was walking in the temple, in the portico of Solomon.* ²⁴*So the Jews gathered around him and said to him, "How long will you keep us in suspense? If you are the Messiah, tell us plainly."* ²⁵*Jesus answered, "I have told you, and you do not believe. The works that I do in my Father's name testify to me;* ²⁶*but you do not believe, because you do not belong to my sheep.* ²⁷*My sheep hear my voice. I know them, and they follow me.* ²⁸*I give them eternal life, and they will never perish. No one will snatch them out of my hand.* ²⁹*What my Father has given me is greater than all else, and no one can snatch it out of the Father's hand.* ³⁰*The Father and I are one."*

³¹*The Jews took up stones again to stone him.* ³²*Jesus replied, "I have shown you many good works from the Father. For which of these are you going to stone me?"* ³³*The Jews answered, "It is not for a good work that we are going to stone you, but for blasphemy, because you, though only a human being, are making yourself God."* ³⁴*Jesus answered, "Is it not written in your law, 'I said, you are gods'?* ³⁵*If those to whom the word of God came were called 'gods'—and the scripture cannot be annulled—*³⁶*can you say that the one whom the Father has*

sanctified and sent into the world is blaspheming because I said, 'I am God's Son'? [37]*If I am not doing the works of my Father, then do not believe me.* [38]*But if I do them, even though you do not believe me, believe the works, so that you may know and understand that the Father is in me and I am in the Father."* [39]*Then they tried to arrest him again, but he escaped from their hands.*

[40]*He went away again across the Jordan to the place where John had been baptizing earlier, and he remained there.* [41]*Many came to him, and they were saying, "John performed no sign, but everything that John said about this man was true."* [42]*And many believed in him there.*

The manifestations of Jesus have occurred during the cycle of Israel's festivals: the Sabbath, the feast of Passover, and the feast of Booths (Tabernacles). Here Jesus is walking and teaching in the temple during yet another Jewish feast, the festival of the Dedication (verse 22). The eight-day feast, known also as Hanukkah, celebrates the rededication of the temple in 164 BC after its desecration by Antiochus Epiphanes and the regaining of Jewish religious freedom, as recounted in the first book of Maccabees. It occurs annually near the time of the winter equinox and is marked by the burning of festive candles.

The question of Jesus' identity remains the primary theme. Despite all that Jesus has taught and all that he has done, those who gathered around him in the temple still do not know who he is. Jesus said, "I have told you, and you do not believe" (verse 25), and "I have shown you many good works from the Father" (verse 32). Jesus had healed a man crippled for 38 years and a man blind from birth. He had fed thousands of people from a few loaves and fish. These are the kinds of things that can be done only with the power and authority of God.

Jesus states that the reason for the unbelief of the Jewish leaders is that they do not belong to his sheep (verse 26). Jesus' portrayal of his sheep is a description of authentic believers: they listen to his voice and they follow him; Jesus knows them and gives them eternal life; and no one can snatch them away from him (verses 27–28). True discipleship is a gift from the Father, and faith in Jesus joins the believer not only to Jesus but also to his Father.

Jesus' words, "The Father and I are one," form the climax of this section of the gospel (verse 30). No longer do the Jews need to look at the temple to see the visible presence of God among them. As the Word Made Flesh, Jesus is the fullness of God's presence among his people. Because of the oneness of the Father and the Son, Jesus can restore life on the Sabbath, proclaim that he is the bread from heaven that perfects the Passover, and declare that he is the living water and light of the world that fulfills the feast of Booths.

The feast of Dedication remembers the sanctification of the temple's altar of sacrifice after its desecration. But Jesus is present at the feast as "the one whom the Father has sanctified and sent into the world" (verse 36). He brings to completion the sign and foreshadowing of Israel's feast of Dedication. The stone altar and magnificent building will be destroyed, but the One sanctified by the Father is the living temple of God's presence in the world. Israel's search for the unseen God finds its goal in the face of Jesus.

As the Jewish leaders attempt to stone Jesus for blasphemy, Jesus left the temple area and returned to the place where John had been baptizing at the beginning of the gospel. The place still echoes with the witness of John the Baptist and many came to believe in Jesus there. The ministry of Jesus has come full circle as this section of the gospel ends. But this return to the beginning suggests that the end is near. The second half of the gospel will recount the events leading to Jesus' death and will narrate his death on the cross and his hour of glory.

As the Christians of John's community read this gospel, they proudly look upon their Jewish heritage and remember God's saving actions commemorated in the feasts of Sabbath, Passover, Booths, and Dedication. The narrative of Jesus' presence at these events affirms that the Old Testament has been perfected, not eliminated. His conflict with the Jewish leaders is not a conflict between Jesus and Israel or between Jesus and Judaism. It is rather a clash with those who have determined that Jesus is not Israel's Messiah, who call him a blasphemer and wish to put him to death. As the Word Made Flesh, Jesus shows the continuity of salvation history as God completes his saving plan in him. God will reveal his own glory by glorifying his Son and drawing all people to himself.

Reflection and Discussion

• In what sense does Jesus bring the Feast of Hanukkah to perfection?

• In what sense should Christians be proud of their Jewish heritage? Why is it so critical that I understand God's works through the Old Testament?

• What have I learned about Jesus and about myself through studying the first half of John's Gospel?

Prayer

Word Made Flesh, I believe that you are the human face of God in my life and in our world. Deepen my faith as I experience you through the inspired gospel, and show me the truth that leads to everlasting life.

SUGGESTIONS FOR FACILITATORS, GROUP SESSION 6

1. Welcome group members and make any final announcements or requests.

2. You may want to pray this prayer as a group:

Revealing God, we believe that Jesus is your human face in our world. As the Word Made Flesh, he declares that he is the bread from heaven that completes the Passover, the living water and light of the world that fulfills the feast of Booths, and the sanctified temple that perfects the feast of Dedication. Open our eyes to see the face of Jesus, and give us the faith that leads to the fullness of life.

3. Ask one or more of the following questions:
   • How has this study of John's gospel enriched your life?
   • In what way has this study challenged you the most?

4. Discuss lessons 25 through 30. Choose one or more of the questions for reflection and discussion from each lesson to discuss as a group.

5. Ask the group if they would like to study another book in the Threshold Bible Study series. Discuss the topic and dates, and make a decision among those interested. Ask the group members to suggest people they would like to invite to participate in the next study series.

6. Ask the group to discuss the insights that stand out most from this study over the past six weeks.

7. Conclude by praying aloud the following prayer or another of your own choosing:

Holy Spirit of the living God, you inspired the writers of the Scriptures, and you have guided our study during these weeks. Continue to deepen our love for the word of God in the holy Scriptures, and draw us more deeply into the heart of Jesus. We thank you for the confident hope you have placed within us and the gifts which build up the church. Through this study, lead us to worship and witness more fully and fervently, and bless us now and always with the fire of your love.

THE **GOSPEL OF JOHN** IN THE SUNDAY LECTIONARY

John 1:1–18
Christmas ABC–Mass during the Day *(16)*

John 1:1–18
Second Sunday after Christmas ABC *(19)*

John 1:6–8, 19–28
Third Sunday of Advent B *(8)*

John 1:29–34
2nd Sunday in OT A *(64)*

John 1:35–42
2nd Sunday in OT B *(65)*

John 2:1–11
2nd Sunday in OT C *(66)*

John 2:13–25
3rd Sunday of Lent B *(29)*

John 3:14–21
4th Sunday of Lent B *(32)*

John 3:16–18
Trinity Sunday A *(164)*

John 4:5–42
3rd Sunday of Lent A *(28)*

John 6:1–15
17th Sunday in OT B *(110)*

John 6:24–35
18th Sunday in OT B *(113)*

John 6:41–51
19th Sunday in OT B *(116)*

John 6:51–58
Body and Blood of Christ A *(167)*

John 6:51–58
20th Sunday in OT B *(119)*

John 6:60–69
21st Sunday in OT B *(122)*

John 7:37–39
Vigil of Pentecost ABC *(62)*

John 8:1–11
5th Sunday of Lent C *(36)*

John 9:1–41
4th Sunday of Lent A *(31)*

John 10:1–10
4th Sunday of Easter A *(49)*

John 10:11–18
4th Sunday of Easter B *(50)*

John 10:27–30
4th Sunday of Easter C *(51)*

John 11:1–45
5th Sunday of Lent A *(34)*

John 12:12–16
Palm Sunday B, Procession with Palms *(37)*

John 12:20–33
5th Sunday of Lent B *(35)*

John 13:1–15
Holy Thursday: Lord's Supper ABC *(39)*

John 13:31–33a, 34–35
5th Sunday of Easter C *(54)*

John 14:1–12
5th Sunday of Easter A *(52)*

John 14:15–21
6th Sunday of Easter A *(55)*

John 14:15–16, 23b–26
Pentecost C *(63)*

John 14:23–29
6th Sunday of Easter C *(57)*

John 15:1–8
5th Sunday of Easter B *(53)*

John 15:9–17
6th Sunday of Easter B *(56)*

John 15:26–27; 16:12–15
Pentecost B *(63)*

John 16:12–15
Trinity Sunday C *(166)*

John 17:1–11a
7th Sunday of Easter A *(59)*

John 17:11b–19
7th Sunday of Easter B *(60)*

John 17:20–26
7th Sunday of Easter C *(61)*

John 18:1—19:42
Good Friday ABC *(40)*

John 18:33b–37
Christ the King B *(161)*

John 19:31–37
Sacred Heart Friday B *(171)*

John 20:1–9
Easter Sunday ABC *(42)*

John 20:19–23
Pentecost Sunday ABC *(63)*

John 20:19–31
2nd Sunday of Easter ABC *(43/44/45)*

John 21:1–19
3rd Sunday of Easter C *(48)*

Ordering Additional Studies

AVAILABLE TITLES IN THIS SERIES INCLUDE...

Advent Light • Angels of God • Eucharist

The Feasts of Judaism • The Holy Spirit and Spiritual Gifts

Jerusalem, the Holy City • The Lamb and the Beasts

Mysteries of the Rosary • The Names of Jesus

People of the Passion • Pilgrimage in the Footsteps of Jesus

The Resurrection and the Life • The Sacred Heart of Jesus

Stewardship of the Earth • The Tragic and Triumphant Cross

Jesus, the Messianic King (Part 1): Matthew 1–16

Jesus, the Messianic King (Part 2): Matthew 17–28

Jesus, the Word Made Flesh (Part 1): John 1–10

Jesus, the Word Made Flesh (Part 2): John 11–21

COMING FALL 2011 Jesus, the Suffering Servant (Part 1): Mark 1–8
Jesus, the Suffering Servant (Part 2): Mark 9–16

Church of the Holy Spirit (Part 1): Acts of the Apostles 1–14
Church of the Holy Spirit (Part 2): Acts of the Apostles 15–28 **COMING 2012**
Jesus, the Compassionate Savior (Part 1): Luke 1–11
Jesus, the Compassionate Savior (Part 2): Luke 12–24

To check availability or for a description
of each study, visit our website at
www.ThresholdBibleStudy.com
or call us at 1-800-321-0411

TWENTY
THIRD *23rd*
PUBLICATIONS